HOLIDAY CAKES AND CUPCAKES

45 FONDANT DESIGNS FOR YEAR-ROUND CELEBRATIONS

3 3113 03087 2503

Published by Tuttle Publishing, an imprint of
Periplus Editions (HK) Ltd

www.tuttlepublishing.com

Library of Congress Cataloging-in-Publication Data

Deacon, Carol.
 Holiday cakes and cupcakes : matching cakes
and cupcakes for year round celebrations / Carol
Deacon.
   p. cm.
 ISBN 978-0-8048-4261-7 (hardcover)
 1. Cake. 2. Cake decorating. I. Title.
 TX771.D426 2012
 641.86'53--dc23

                        2011052612

 ISBN 978-0-8048-4261-7

Distributed by
North America, Latin America & Europe
Tuttle Publishing
364 Innovation Drive
North Clarendon, VT 05759-9436 U.S.A.
Tel: 1 (802) 773-8930; Fax: 1 (802) 773-6993
info@tuttlepublishing.com
www.tuttlepublishing.com

Japan
Tuttle Publishing
Yaekari Building, 3rd Floor
5-4-12 Osaki
Shinagawa-ku, Tokyo 141 0032
Tel: (81) 3 5437-0171; Fax: (81) 3 5437-0755
sales@tuttle.co.jp
www.tuttle.co.jp

Asia Pacific
Berkeley Books Pte. Ltd.
61 Tai Seng Avenue #02-12
Singapore 534167
Tel: (65) 6280-1330; Fax: (65) 6280-6290
inquiries@periplus.com.sg
www.periplus.com

15 14 13 12   8 7 6 5 4 3 2 1

Printed in Singapore   1204 CP

For Tory Brettell, Jane Duncan (Buckler),
Libby Griffin (Mayall), Sally Hodgson (Spalding),
Jane Munro (Glasgow), and all the rest of our
year at Droitwich High School as we all have
BIG birthdays this year and deserve a cake!

And Jill Hindle, Penny Hollingsworth (Dunn)
and Sally Siviter and who didn't go to Droitwich
High School but might as well have!

To my great mates!

Contents

INTRODUCTION

Putting this book together it struck me once more how incredibly versatile a cake can be. Cakes are used to celebrate all sorts of important family and social occasions including weddings, birthdays and holidays and virtually all cultures have cake in some form or another. There are hundreds of recipes and flavors, some going back centuries and, as for ways to decorate a cake, there must be thousands if not millions of ways. Whether you enjoy cake or not, it really is a unique and special foodstuff that can be used to celebrate practically anything.

In this book, I've tried to put together a collection of cakes for high days and holidays. Special days when you might have a group of friends or family around. I wanted to give you designs that would make your friends both gasp in amazement and giggle with delight when they see the masterpiece you have created. If you're new to cake decorating or a little nervous then I hope that the lasting memories, pictures, and gratitude that should follow your cake's unveiling will outweigh any stress that goes into its creation.

Read through a recipe before you begin as sometimes suggestions are made along the way which you might like to take into account before you begin. Also try to plan ahead to make things easier for yourself. A sponge needed in two weeks time could be baked today and frozen until required. A fondant model for the top of the cake can be made well in advance and kept until needed. Actually I should really do what I write. I'm going on holiday next week. The week after I come back I have a wedding cake to do. It's quite a fun one – bride and groom on top – and the bride's horse scrabbling up the side of the cake. I keep telling myself to get on and get the horse done before I go away but...

Anyway, less of my incompetence! I hope you will enjoy using this book time and time again. Whatever the celebratory reason that leads you to create a cake, I hope you have a fantastic party and that your cake is the center of attention.

Fondant wishes!

Carol Deacon

BASIC EQUIPMENT

Go into any cake decorating shop and you'll be amazed at how much "stuff" is available. Here are the basics that will allow you to make the cakes in this book.

1. Baking Tray or Cookie Sheet For baking cookies

2. Sieve Use this for sieving flour or confectioners' sugar and sprinkling "snow" over Christmas cakes. You can also push fondant through it to make hair or foliage.

3. Wooden Spoon For use when making cake batter by hand. You can also use the handle to poke large hollows into your models.

4. Mixing Bowl

5. Cooling Rack Place your baked cakes and cookies on this to speed up the cooling process.

6. Spatula The flexible head on this utensil will let you scrape every last drop of cake batter or frosting out of your mixing bowl.

Cheeky Straw

7. Palette knife This is a special blunt knife with a bendy metal blade designed for spreading soft frosting easily.

8. Pastry brush Use this to dab water on boards and apply jam on to your fruitcakes.

9. & 10. Piping Bag & Nozzles (Tips) A large fabric bag and a large star nozzle makes piping elegant cupcakes easy. Smaller nozzles are for finer piping work. The smaller the number the smaller the hole at the tip. I would usually use these with a paper piping bag. You can also use the nozzles to press curved smiles into fondant characters or as mini circle cutters.

11. Cutters For cutting simple shapes out of cookie dough or fondant.

12. Measuring Cups Useful if you like to cook using cup measurements.

13. Paint Brushes A soft medium brush that won't dent the fondant when you stick sections together and a fine tipped brush for lettering or making eyeballs.

14. Cheeky Straw This is simply an ordinary drinking straw with a little bit cut off one end at an angle. With this end you can press miniature "U" shapes into fondant so it's ideal for giving your characters cheeks. Use the other uncut end as a tiny circle cutter or for pressing little circles into your fondant.

15. Carving Knife You will use this for slicing your cakes to make them ready for decorating.

16. Small, Sharp, Non-Serrated Knife Essential for cutting fondant cleanly and smoothly.

17. Mini Rolling Pin It's easier to roll out little bits of fondant using a smaller rolling pin. If you don't have one, use a paint-brush instead.

18. Large Rolling Pin For rolling out fondant and marzipan (almond paste).

19. Scissors For cutting ribbon, string, baking paper, edible wafer paper, and fondant Christmas trees!

20. Scalpel (Craft Knife) Useful for cutting out tiny bits of fondant and giving you characters long luscious eyelashes.

21. Turntable Once you have got one of these you will wonder how you managed without one. Placing a cake on the turntable will bring it up to a manageable working height. You can turn the cake around easily when working, which is useful when it's a large, heavy cake.

22. Cup Cake Baking Tray These are for baking cupcakes.

23. Cake Boards & Cards A cake board is a food-safe, light, yet durable, board that won't bend or break no matter how heavy your cake. Cake cards are thinner and are ideal for small fondant models.

24. Cake Smoother This is how you get your fondant cake covering flat and smooth. You use it a bit like an iron to level any lumps and bumps.

25. Tape Measure Useful for measuring round tins and cakes for paper linings and ribbons.

26. Circle Cutters You will find a set of these really useful as cut out circles are used often. You can always use a lid instead but it's always a fiddle finding one the right size.

27. Toothpicks (Cocktail Sticks) Use these for adding food color to fondant and little dot eyes on your characters. Don't use them for internal model supports as they could cause injury if eaten. Use a strand of raw uncooked spaghetti instead.

28. Scales These are for weighing ingredients

29. Baking Pan (Tin) These are for baking your cakes.

BAKING A DELICIOUS CAKE

It doesn't matter how grand a cake looks on the outside, it needs to taste good on the inside too. The following three recipes for Madeira sponge (similar to pound cake), chocolate, and a rich fruit cake all produce cakes that are strong enough to carve into shapes and support the sometimes quite weighty frosting; but they are moist and soft when eaten. It may be that you have your own family favorites that work for you. If so, feel free to substitute your own recipes and, if you think others might like them, feel free to send me the recipe!

Flour

Apart from the rich fruitcake, I always use self-rising flour in my cakes. This is flour that already contains a rising agent to help your cakes reach spectacular heights when baked. Flour does vary slightly from country to country and very similar products are called self-raising or cake flour.

If you wish, you can make your own self-rising flour using plain (all purpose) flour and baking powder.

Mix 1 1/2 teaspoons of baking powder and 1 cup (150g) of plain (all purpose) flour together. Double or triple these amounts if you need more for your recipe.

A friend of mine who runs an American cake shop mentioned recently that she sometimes gets customers complaining that a recipe they have used for ages suddenly doesn't work. The problem is usually the flour, which they have measured in cups. Flour contains oil and if it is old, the oil dries out and becomes lighter. This is where a set of scales will help (and they don't have to be expensive ones). Try redoing the recipe this time weighing the flour. If the flour is old and lighter, you may find you actually need to use more to achieve the weight your recipe requires.

There is also a wealth of information on the Internet about flour, how it varies and what may work best for you in your part of the world.

Superfine (Caster) Sugar

For sponge cakes and chocolate cakes superfine (caster) sugar is best. Superfine sugar granules are finer than normal everyday granulated sugar and will produce a slightly lighter cake. However, it is perfectly fine to use granulated sugar if that's all you have. It will still produce a cake that is tasty and delicious.

Brown Sugar

There are all sorts of brown sugars, but for the fruit cake I use dark brown soft sugar as it produces a darker colored cake. When fresh it should be slightly damp. You can use lighter colored sugar if you prefer although I would avoid turbinado (or demerara or "raw") sugar as it has an odd and distinctive taste. Make sure you seal the packet well after using brown sugar or it will solidify into an unuseable solid sugar brick! You can make your own brown sugar by mixing white granulated sugar with molasses. Use one tablespoon of molasses to every cup of white sugar.

Butter and Margarine

There are many types of specialist baking fats and margarines available, but for baking I always use butter, so I've specified butter in all the baking recipes. You are perfectly free to substitute something else you prefer. However, read the packaging as some of the low fat spreads cannot be used for baking. The one area I would never use anything other than butter is buttercream and, actually, I personally prefer lightly salted to unsalted butter—but again it's a question of personal taste. I would never use margarine to make buttercream. I don't like the taste of it and also some of the very soft margarines are designed not to harden and therefore don't hold their shapes particularly well.

White Fat

Now I know that cake decorators in countries such as the USA have been using white fat for years to produce white icing. We have white vegetable fats here in the UK but it's something we don't normally

use in this way. However, when you need a bright white, soft frosting, normal buttercream just won't do, it simply isn't white enough. So I started to invesigate easy white icings (frostings). There are different methods and ways of making white frostings, but by far the easiest way was simply to substitute white fat for butter in the buttercream recipe. I found I could buy white vegetable fat that contained no hydrogenated vegetable oil, no "e" numbers and no colors or preservatives and that it produced a good white icing. So go on Britain—try it!

Scales and Mixers
If you are serious about baking, I would strongly recommend that you buy a set of scales—they don't have to be expensive. They will allow you to use recipes (and not just baking ones) from all over the world easily and correctly without resorting to guesswork. And as I mentioned in the flour section above, weighing your flour, especially if it's a bit old, could save you from a flat disaster!

It's the same with mixers. If you make cakes and frosting regularly, I would really recommend buying one. I have owned a large free standing mixer (which I have polished up for its moment of fame here in this book) for many years now and it just makes life so much simpler. Tip the (weighed!) ingredients in, switch it on and off it goes. However, I do appreciate that big mixers like mine are expensive so if you're just starting out, invest in a cheap hand held one—I did. You can use it for other things too—whipping cream or making pancake batter for example.

LINING A CAKE PAN

Okay, I'll admit it, lining a cake pan is pretty boring but it will ensure that your cake comes out all in one piece.

Fruit Cake Pans

Lining a pan for a fruitcake is really important to prevent the sides and base from scorching during its long baking time.

Measure the height and circumference of the pan and cut four lengths of waxed, greaseproof, or baking paper to that length and just wider than the height of the pan. Place to one side. Standing the pan on the paper, draw round the base three times and depending upon what shape pan you are using cut out a three discs or squares. Cut a small hole into the center of one of them. Wrap two of the long sections around the outside of the pan and hold in place with a string (don't use plastic string). Make a fold along the long edge of the two remaining long strips and cut a fringe into it. Rub a little butter around the inside of the pan and stand the long strips inside. The fringes should allow the strips to stand upright and fit right into the edges of the pan. Place the two whole base sections into the bottom of the pan.

Fill the pan two thirds full with fruit cake mixture and rest the remaining bit of paper with the hole on top. The hole will allow steam to escape while it's cooking.

Sponge or Chocolate Cake Pans

To line a pan for a sponge or chocolate cake, rub a little butter around the inside of the pan to hold the lining in place. Measure the circumference of the tin and cut a strip of waxed, greaseproof, or baking paper long enough to stand around the outside of the pan and wide enough so that when it's standing it's just a little higher than the top of the pan. Stand the pan on the paper and draw round the base. Cut out your circle or square. Stand the strip of paper around the inside of the pan and place the base section in the bottom.

> **TIP:** *Remember not every cake has to be an all singing, all dancing one. There's immense pleasure to be found in a simple slice of sponge cake with jam and buttercream.*

Using Baked Bean Cans

It's amazing what you can bake a cake in! I have used a collection of small cans like these to bake a mass order of mini Christmas cakes. We all ate baked beans for weeks and it was a bit fiddly to do but it saved a lot of wastage cutting small round cakes out of larger ones.

Wash the tin and rub a little butter around the insides of the can. Measure the circumference of the tin and cut a strip of waxed paper to that length and just wider than the height of the tin. Trace around the base and cut out a disc. Stand the long strip inside the tin and place the disc into the bottom.

For the Firework on page 36, I baked a little cake in a small baked bean can. Wash the can and line it as described above. Mix up a 2 or 3-egg Madeira mix using the recipe chart (page 16) and fill the tin two-thirds full. I used the rest of the batter to make a heap of cupcakes. Bake in the middle of the oven for about 20 minutes.

TIP: *If you really can't bear lining a pan, you can buy ready made paper linings from kitchen or cake decoration equipment shops. Quick release sprays are also available. Finally, there is also silicone bakeware that require no lining and come in many funky colors.*

Shallow Sandwich Cake Pans

When using a sandwich pan you only need to line the base. Place the pan onto waxed paper, draw round the base, and cut out a disc. Grease the base and sides of the pan and place the disc in the bottom of the pan.

For the Christening Cake on page 30, I used two 7-inch (18 cm) round sandwich pans. Use the 3-egg Madeira mix from the recipe chart. Grease the pans and place a disc of waxed paper in the base to stop the cake from sticking. Mix the batter up in one batch then divide the mixture between the two pans. Bake in the middle of the oven at 300°F (150°C) for 25-30 minutes until the cakes are golden and starting to pull away from the sides.

Tip the cakes out onto a cooling rack and peel off the waxed paper and allow to cool.

Storing and Freezing Your Cakes

You can begin to decorate the chocolate or Madeira cakes as soon as they're cooled. Once they come out of the oven let them sit for a few minutes then turn the tin over and tip them out onto a cooling rack. You can either remove the paper they were baked in to speed up the cooling process or leave it in place.

If you don't want to decorate them straight away, cover them with plastic wrap once they're cooled and decorate the following day. There is actually an advantage to doing this—the cake will be slightly firmer and easier to work with.

If you wish to freeze either the sponge or chocolate cakes, bind them in plastic wrap when cool and freeze for up to three months. Defrost at room temperature for a few hours before decorating.

Fruitcake takes a long time to cool down, anything up to eight hours depending on its size and room temperature. Leave it in the pan while it cools so it doesn't lose its shape. Once it has cooled it can be decorated.

If you wish to store the fruitcake before decorating it, turn it out of the pan but leave it in the paper. Pierce the top a few times with a skewer or toothpick (cocktail stick) and drizzle a couple of tablespoons of brandy over the top. Wrap the cake in two lots of waxed (greaseproof) paper and two lots of tin foil. It will keep quite happily like this for three months, its flavors deepening and maturing as it does so. If you wish you can "feed" it every week by drizzling a little extra brandy over it and re-wrapping it. Once a fruitcake has been marzipanned and iced it is then sealed and airtight. It should keep for at least a couple of months at room temperature in a cardboard cake box.

A sponge cake that has been covered in buttercream can be frozen (unless the sponge or buttercream has been frozen already in which case it cannot be re-frozen). Bind in plastic wrap and freeze for up to three months.

Cakes covered using fondant cannot be frozen, refrigerated, or kept in a plastic food box because these storage methods will make the fondant "sweat" and go soggy.

If you have covered your sponge or chocolate cake with fondant you should be able to keep it for 4-5 days. Ideally, keep it in a cardboard cake box free from flies and dust.

MADEIRA SPONGE CAKE RECIPES

This is a simple all-in-one recipe. Throw everything into the bowl together and mix. Read the section on flour beforehand and do try to use scales. If you find the cake is not rising well because the flour you in your area is heavier, add a little baking powder to the mix to give it a hand.

1 Grease and line your cake pan (see page 14) and preheat your oven to 300°F (150°C)
2 If you are using a mixer, sift your flour into the bowl and add the rest of the ingredients. Mix on the slowest speed to gently bind the ingredients together. Switch to the mixer's highest speed and beat all the ingredients for a minute until the mixture is pale and smooth.
3 If you are mixing by hand, make sure your butter is very soft (place it in a microwave for a few seconds if necessary). Then beat the butter and sugar together until creamy. Add the eggs and beat those in too until the mixture is smooth. Sift the flour and gently stir it in with a metal spoon.
4 Spoon the mixture into your prepared pan and smooth the top. Place the cake in the center of the pre-heated oven and bake for the required time. Not all ovens bake the same so the baking times are approximate. Your cake will be ready when it is starting to pull away from the sides and you can't hear bubbling noises. To check for sure, insert a knife or metal skewer. If it comes out clean then the cake is done. If there's mixture on the skewer, cook for another five or ten minutes or so.

Variations This is a very versatile recipe which lends itself to all sorts of variations. To alter the flavor, stir in a tablespoon of cocoa or coffee to create a simple chocolate or coffee cake. Add a dash of almond or mint flavoring for something unexpected. Add a handful of desiccated coconut, a ripe banana (mashed). You could even add the zest of an orange or lemon. To make a colorful cake stir in a little food coloring before baking. Perhaps add a little green food color to your Halloween cake for example. If you just stir it in lightly, your cake will have a marbled appearance when baked. Stir it in thoroughly and your cake will be one solid color. You can even alter your cake's texture by stirring in chocolate beans or chocolate chips, raisins, or glacé cherries.

For Square Pans	6-inch 15 cm	7-inch 18 cm	8-inch 20 cm	9-inch 23 cm	10-inch 25 cm	11-inch 28 cm	12-inch 30 cm
For Round Pans	6-inch 15 cm	7-inch 18 cm	8-inch 20 cm	9-inch 23 cm	10-inch 25 cm	11-inch 28 cm	12-inch 30 cm
Self-rising Flour	1¹/₂ cups 6 oz 170 g	2 cups 8 oz 225 g	2³/₄ cups 12 oz 340 g	3¹/₂ cups 1 lb 450 g	4 cups 1 lb 2 oz 500 g	4¹/₂ cups 1 lb 4 oz 570 g	5 cups 1lb 6 oz 625 g	6 cups 1lb 10 oz 735 g
Butter	¹/₂ cup 4 oz 115 g 1 stick	³/₄ cup 6 oz 170 g 1¹/₂ sticks	1¹/₄ cups 10 oz 285 g 2¹/₂ sticks	1³/₄ cups 14 oz 400 g 3¹/₂ sticks	2 cups 1 lb 450 g 4 sticks	2¹/₄ cups 1 lb 2 oz 500 g 4¹/₂ sticks	2¹/₂ cups 1 lb 4 oz 550 g 5 sticks	3 cups 1 lb 8 oz 700 g 6 sticks
Sugar (superfine)	¹/₂ cup 4 oz 115 g	³/₄ cup 6 oz 170 g	1¹/₄ cups 10 oz 285 g	1³/₄ cups 14 oz 400 g	2 cups 1 lb 450 g	2¹/₄ cups 1 lb 2 oz 500 g	2¹/₂ cups 1 lb 4 oz 570 g	3 cups 1 lb 8 oz 700 g
Eggs	2	3	5	7	8	9	10	12
Milk	1 tbsp	1 tbsp	2 tbsps	3 tbsps	4 tbsps	5 tbsps	5 tbsps	6 tbsps
Baking Time	1 hr	1–1¹/₂ hrs	1¹/₂–2 hrs	1¹/₂–2¹/₄ hrs	2 hrs	2 hrs	2–2¹/₂ hrs	2–2¹/₂ hrs

CHOCOLATE CAKE RECIPES

This is an excellent chocolate cake for a special ocassion. It has a strong yet velvety texture that is easy to cut into shapes. You will need to use a mixer that has a whisk attachment as well as a normal beater. If you don't possess one or simply want to make a less complicated cake, use the Madeira cake recipe but add cocoa powder to it. As it bakes, a hard crust will form on top that may scorch or crack. This is normal. Slice it off and discard the crust once the cake has cooled and before you decorate it.

For Square Pans		6-inch 15 cm	7-inch 18 cm	8-inch 20 cm	9-inch 23 cm	10-inch 25 cm	11-inch 28 cm	12-inch 30 cm
For Round Pans	6-inch 15 cm	7-inch 18 cm	8-inch 20 cm	9-inch 23 cm	10-inch 25 cm	11-inch 28 cm	12-inch 30 cm	
Semisweet Chocolate	5 oz 150 g	6 oz 175 g	8 oz 225 g	10 oz 275 g	12 oz 350 g	14 oz 400 g	1 lb 450 g	1 lb 2 oz 500 g
Butter	$^1/_3$ cup 3 oz 90 g $^3/_4$ stick	$^1/_2$ cup 4 oz 120 g 1 stick	$^3/_4$ cup 6 oz 175 g 1$^1/_2$ sticks	1 cup 8 oz 250 g 2 sticks	1$^1/_4$ cups 10 oz 285 g 2$^1/_2$ sticks	1$^1/_2$ cups 12 oz 350 g 3 sticks	1$^3/_4$ cups 14 oz 400 g 3$^1/_2$ sticks	2 cups 1 lb 450 g 4 sticks
Sugar (superfine)	$^1/_5$ cup 1$^1/_2$ oz 45 g	$^1/_3$ cup 2$^1/_2$ oz 75 g	$^1/_2$ cup 4 oz 120 g	$^2/_3$ cup 5 oz 150 g	$^3/_4$ cup 6 oz 175 g	$^9/_{10}$ cup 7 oz 200 g	1 cup 8 oz 250 g	1$^1/_5$ cups 9 oz 275 g
Eggs (separated)	3	4	6	8	10	12	14	16
Self-rising Flour	$^3/_5$ cup 3 oz 90 g	$^9/_{10}$ cup 4 oz 120 g	1$^1/_4$ cups 6 oz 175 g	1$^4/_5$ cups 8 oz 250 g	2$^1/_4$ cups 10 oz 285 g	2$^3/_4$ cups 12 oz 350 g	3$^1/_4$ cups 14 oz 400 g	3$^3/_4$ cups 1 lb 450 g
Confectioners' Sugar (icing)	$^1/_5$ cup 1 oz 30 g	$^1/_3$ cup 1$^1/_2$ oz 45 g	$^1/_2$ cup 2 oz 60 g	$^2/_3$ cup 3 oz 90 g	$^3/_4$ cup 3$^1/_2$ oz 100 g	1$^1/_{10}$ cups 4$^1/_2$ oz 130 g	1$^1/_5$ cups 5 oz 150 g	1$^1/_3$ cups 6 oz 175 g
Baking Time	45 mins	45 mins–1 hr	1 hr	1–1$^1/_4$ hrs	1–1$^1/_4$ hrs	1$^1/_4$–1$^1/_2$ hrs	1$^1/_4$–1$^3/_4$ hrs	1$^1/_4$–2 hrs

1 Pre-heat your oven to 350°F (180°C) . Line your cake pan (see page 14) and separate the eggs placing the whites and yolks in two different bowls.

2 Melt the chocolate in a large bowl and place to one side.

3 Beat the butter and sugar together using the normal beater on the mixer until fluffy.

4 Beat in the egg yolks. Tip the chocolate into the mixture and keep the bowl the chocolate was melted in. Bind the mixture together on a slow speed.

5 Gently stir in the sifted flour using a metal spoon then scrape the chocolate mixture back into the chocolate bowl. Remove the beater from the mixer.

6 Wash your machine's mixing bowl. Dry it and place the egg whites into it.

7 Place the whisking element on your mixer. Whisk the egg whites until stiff then whisk in the confectioners' sugar. Remove the whisk and put the beater attachment back on.

8 Tip the chocolate mixture into the egg whites and mix together on a slow speed. It will look dreadful at first but the two will mix smoothly together eventually.

9 Scrape the mixture into the prepared pan and bake immediately.

10 When the cake is ready there will be no bubbling noises. To be sure, insert a knife or metal skewer. (You may have to cut a small chunk out of the cake's crust to do this). If it comes out clean, then the cake is done. If there's mixture on the skewer, cook for a little longer.

> **TIP:** *Unless you have a very big mixer, it may be easier to make the largest sizes in two separate batches then gently stir together. Have everything weighed out beforehand though as this mixture needs to be cooked immediately.*

RECIPES FOR ENGLISH-STYLE FRUITCAKE

In the UK, it is traditional to have a rich fruitcake for Christmas. The dried fruits should be soaked overnight in brandy or fruit juice before cooking so that they're plump and moist. The cake should be made in October to allow it time to mature and for the flavors to develop... In the real world, even if you just threw this cake together on Christmas Eve with fruit straight out of a packet, you should still end up with a cake that is tasty and moist plus a house full of spicy Christmas aromas.

For Square Pans	6-inch 15 cm	7-inch 18 cm	8-inch 20 cm	9-inch 23 cm	10-inch 25 cm	11-inch 28 cm	12-inch 30 cm
For Round Pans	6-inch 15 cm	7-inch 18 cm	8-inch 20 cm	9-inch 23 cm	10-inch 25 cm	11-inch 28 cm	12-inch 30 cm
Golden Raisins (sultanas), Currants, Raisins (each)	3 oz 90 g	4½ oz 135 g	6 oz 175 g	8 oz 250 g	12 oz 350 g	1 lb 450 g	1 lb 4 oz 550 g	1 lb 8 oz 700 g
Mixed Peel	⅔ oz 20 g	1 oz 30 g	1½ oz 45 g	2 oz 60 g	2½ oz 75 g	3½ oz 100 g	4 oz 120 g	6 oz 175 g
Glacé Cherries (halved)	1½ oz 45 g	2 oz 60 g	2½ oz 75 g	4 oz 120 g	5 oz 150 g	7 oz 200 g	8 oz 250 g	10 oz 300 g
Brandy (for soaking)	2 tbsp	2 tbsp	3 tbsp	3 tbsp	4 tbsp	6 tbsp	6 tbsp	8 tbsp
Eggs	2	3	4	6	8	10	12	15
Soft dark brown sugar	½ cup 3 oz 90 g	¾ cup 4½ oz 135 g	¾ cup 6 oz 175 g	1 cup 8 oz 250 g	2 cups 12 oz 350 g	2¼ cups 1 lb 450 g	3 cups 1 lb 4 oz 550 g	3½ cups 1½ lb 700 g
All purpose (plain) flour	7/10 cup 3 oz 90 g	1 1/10 cup 4½ oz 135 g	1⅖ cups 6 oz 175 g	2 cups 8 oz 250 g	2⅘ cups 12 oz 350 g	2⅗ cups 1 lb 450 g	4⅖ cups 1 lb 4 oz 550 g	5⅗ cups 1½ lb 700 g
Apple pie spice mixed spice and cinnamon	½ tsp	½ tsp	1 tsp	1 tsp	2 tsp	2 tsp	3 tsp	3 tsp
Lemon Zest	½	1	1	2	2	2	3	3
Ground Almonds and Slivered Almonds	⅔ oz 20 g	1 oz 30 g	1½ oz 45 g	2 oz 60 g	2½ oz 75 g	3½ oz 100 g	4 oz 120 g	5 oz 150 g
Butter	⅓ cup 3 oz 90 g ¾ stick	½ cup 4½ oz 135 g 1 stick	¾ cup 6 oz 175 g 1½ sticks	1 cup 8 oz 250 g 2 sticks	1½ cups 12 oz 350 g 3 sticks	2 cups 1 lb 450 g 4 sticks	2½ cups 1 lb 4 oz 550 g 5 sticks	3 cups 1½ lb 700 g 6 sticks
Baking Time	1½ hrs	1½–2 hrs	2 hrs	2¼ hrs	2½ hrs	3 hrs	3 hrs	3 hrs

1 Line both the inside and outside of your cake pan. (See page 14 for how to do this)
2 Pre-heat the oven to 300°F (150°C)
3 Beat the butter and sugar together until they are soft and creamy. Then beat in the eggs one at a time.
4 Sift the flour and spices into the bowl and gently stir them. Stir in the ground almonds. If you are using a mixer, use the slowest speed. If you're mixing by hand use a metal spoon.
5 Stir the lemon zest and slivered almonds into the soaked dried fruit. Tip the fruits into the cake batter and stir in by hand.
6 Close your eyes and make a wish.
7 Spoon the mixture into the prepared pan and gently smooth the top.
8 Place the disc of waxed paper with the hole cut out on the top of the mixture. Don't press, just let it lie on top.
9 Place the cake in the center of the pre-heated oven and bake. Remove the paper off the top about 15 minutes before it's due to be done. Lightly prod the top of the cake, if it feels very soft and you can still hear a lot of bubbling it is not cooked. If it looks done and feels firm to the touch and is silent, insert a skewer or sharp knife. If it comes out clean – the cake is cooked. If it's not, give it another 15 minutes of cooking and test again. All ovens vary so don't panic if yours cooks in a shorter/longer time than that suggested.
10 Allow the cake to cool completely in the pan before turning out.

MICROWAVE CAKES

If you need to bake a cake really quickly, a microwave cake may be the answer. They will look a little pale and interesting when cooked because they won't have browned on top but nobody will notice once they're covered with frosting. These amounts are for a 7-inch (18 cm) round microwave baking pans. Don't use your normal metal one.

Microwave Vanilla Sponge Cake

1/2 cup (120 g) butter
1/2 cup (120 g) superfine (caster) sugar
2 large eggs
1 teaspoon vanilla extract
3/4 cup (120 g) self-rising flour
1/2 teaspoon baking powder

1 Grease the pan or bowl and place a disc of greaseproof paper in the base.
2 Beat the butter and sugar together until creamy.
3 Beat in the eggs and vanilla extract.
4 Sift the flour and baking powder together and stir in.
5 Scrape into the prepared pan and bake on full for four minutes.

6 Let stand for 10 minutes. Slide a knife around the pan edges to turn the cake out.

Microwave Chocolate Sponge Cake

1/2 cup (120 g) butter
1/2 cup (120 g) superfine (caster) sugar
2 large eggs
2/3 cup (90 g) self-rising flour
2 tablespoons cocoa powder
1/2 teaspoon baking powder

1 Follow steps 1-3 as above leaving out the vanilla extract.
2 Sieve and sift the flour, baking powder, and cocoa powder together into the mixture and gently stir in. Then follow steps 5 and 6 as above.

STOCK SYRUP

If your sponge cake is not going to be eaten as quickly as you'd like, you can add a little stock syrup to the sponge to ensure it stays nice and moist. It's made of sugar dissolved in water and is dabbed onto the cake sponge before frosting.

1 Place 1/2 cup (100 g) of superfine (caster) sugar and 2/3 cup (150ml) of water into a saucepan and stir together.
2 Bring to a boil and simmer for about 5 minutes until the sugar has dissolved.
3 Alternatively, place the ingredients into a heatproof bowl and microwave for a couple of minutes until the sugar is dissolved.
4 Allow the mixture to cool before using. It will keep in a container in the fridge for up to a week.

How to Use Stock Syrup
When you are ready to ice your cake, slice the cake horizontally into layers as normal. Before applying the buttercream, lightly dab some stock syrup over the top of each slice using a soft pastry brush. Do not saturate the sponge or you'll end up with trifle. Then spread buttercream over the layers and assemble your cake as normal.

CHOCOLATE CAKE POPS

This is a delicious way of using up the bits of cake you're left with when you slice the top off a cake to level it or a bit of cake that is perhaps just a little bit past its best. In fact, they are so scrumptious and easy that you may find yourself baking a cake just to destroy it to make a large batch!

1 You can use a combination of any type of chocolate—milk, semi-sweet (plain), or white and any type of cake—Madeira, chocolate, or fruit.

2 Crumble the cake in a bowl into and weigh it. Use about 1 ounce (30 g) of chocolate to every 1 ounce (30 g) of cake crumb. Then weigh out the same amount of chocolate. So if you have 4 ounces (120 g) of crumbs you need 4 ounces (120 g) of chocolate.

3 Melt the chocolate and stir in the cake crumbs. Allow it to cool slightly then roll it into little ball shapes. Stand them on baking sheets and poke a lollipop stick into the top of each one. Refrigerate for about an hour to help the chocolate set or place in the freezer for about 15 minutes.

4 Now, if you sample one at this point you will discover immediately that they taste delicious plain (Madeira cake with white chocolate is my own personal favorite) but you can also decorate them with melted chocolate, sprinkles, or anything else that takes your fancy. The ones shown here were dipped in a mixture of milk and white chocolate.

Melting Chocolate

It's easy to melt chocolate, the secret is not to get any water into it or it will turn gritty. So if you are washing up a bowl prior to using it, make sure you dry it really well.

In the Microwave

Break the chocolate into squares and place in a heatproof non-metallic bowl. Place the bowl into the microwave and heat on full power for about a minute. Give it a stir and repeat in 30-second bursts until the chocolate has melted.

On the Stove top

Break the chocolate into squares and place in a heatproof bowl. Place the bowl on top of a saucepan of gently simmering water. The base of the bowl should not be touching the water. Stir occasionally until the chocolate has melted.

CHOCOLATE CRISPY MIXTURE

This is just the easiest tea time treat to put together and the recipe I always turn to when one of the children mentions at bedtime that "Oh I forgot to tell you, school's having a cake sale tomorrow." Simply melt some chocolate, stir in some cereal and that's it. You can then spoon it into cupcake cases or as done with the Thanksgiving Turkey Cupcake on page 55 create a massive chocolate crispy dome which caused unbelievable excitement amongst those under five foot in the Deacon kitchen!

You will need approximately 3 ounces (90 g) of cereal to every 7 ounces (200 g) of chocolate. If you are making small chocolate crispy cupcakes you could also add some mini marshmallows, chocolate beans or anything else that takes your fancy. Even a handful of dried raisins will add an interesting twist.

COOKIES

Cookies are an easy way to provide three-dimensional support for decorations such as the flowers and hearts on the Summer Holiday Flowers (page 52) and Valentine Heart cakes (page 48). I have used a very basic cookie dough mix but don't let that fool you—there's nothing basic about the taste—they're really quite wonderful just on their own.

9/10 cup (200 g) superfine sugar (caster)
9/10 cup (200 g) butter (softened)
1/2 teaspoon of vanilla essence
1 medium egg (beaten)
3 1/5 cups (400 g) all purpose flour (plain)
Additional flour or confectioners' sugar
    (icing sugar) for rolling out the dough on

1 Beat the sugar, butter, and vanilla together.
2 Slowly add the egg, beating it in as you go.
3 Add the flour and knead the mixture into a dough.
4 If you have time, place in plastic wrap and chill in the refrigerator for a couple of hours before rolling out. This is to help stop the cookie dough spreading out too much in the oven.
4 (again) If like me you haven't left enough time for chilling, use immediately. Don't roll it out too thickly and hope for the best!
5 Dust your work surface with flour (or confectioners' sugar if you prefer a sweeter cookie). Roll out the dough and cut out your shapes.
6 Place onto a greased baking sheet and cook for 8-10 minutes at 350° F (180°C). Place the cookies onto a cooling rack when baked and allow to cool before decorating.

MAKING YOUR CUPCAKES

There are many recipes for making cupcakes but the Madeira recipe on page 16 works perfectly well. The 2–egg mixture will make about 12 cupcakes so double or triple the amounts if you need more. Feel free to add chocolate chips, dried fruit, or even a dash of food coloring if you wish.

1 Pre-heat the oven to 300°F (150° C) and place your cupcake cases into the baking tray. Nowadays there's a huge range of paper and foil cupcake cases available in all sorts of fancy colors and designs. You can also buy silicon cases which are very bright, colorful and also re-useable.
2 Mix up the batter.
3 Spoon the batter into the cupcake cases. The easiest way to do this is using two teaspoons. Use one to scoop a spoonful of batter out of the bowl. Use the other to push it off the first spoon into the cake case. Doing it this way should also stop your fingers from getting sticky. Fill the cake case about two thirds full.
4 Bake for about 25 minutes until the cakes are golden and springy to the touch.

DECORATING YOUR CUPCAKES

There are many ways to decorate your cupcakes once they're cooled and your kitchen is full of their freshly baked aroma. Here are a few suggestions.

Glacé Icing

This is a simple mixture of water and confectioners' (icing) sugar. The amount given here should cover 12 cupcakes or the top of a 7-inch (18 cm) round cake so double the amounts given if you need more. Top the frosted cupcake with half a cherry and you have a cupcake classic.

1 cup (125 g) confectioners' (icing) sugar
1 tablespoon water

1 Sift the icing sugar into a bowl.
2 Add the water and stir together. If it is too thick, add a little more water one drop at a time.
3 Substitute lemon juice for the water for a sweet alternative with a tangy kick or add a dash of food color for a pale pastel alternative.

DECORATING WITH BUTTERCREAM

1 A bowl of buttercream and a piping bag with a large star nozzle fitted into it is a really easy way to make a plain cupcake something quite stunning.

2 Starting from the outside of the cupcake, pipe a swirl around the outside. Continue round and round, moving in towards the center. To finish, loosen your pressure on the bag, poke the tip of the nozzle gently into the buttercream and pull upwards. The buttercream should break away from the piping nozzle leaving a point behind.

3 If you don't have a piping bag, a luscious dollop of buttercream lovingly spread over the top of the cupcake with a palette knife can still exert a longing pull on the tastebuds. Sprinkle on a few edible silver balls, sprinkles, or rice paper flowers and it's ready to party.

Butterflies

I remember my grandmother making these and despite all the technological advances we've made since her day, I still believe the butterfly cake has an important place in modern society and shouldn't be forgotten. Cut a circle of cake out of the top of the cupcake. Place a spoonful of buttercream, and jam too if you wish, onto the top of the cupcake. Slice the cut out section in half and place on top of the cake so that they look like butterfly wings.

Fondant

Dab a little jam (apricot is ideal as it does not have too strong a taste). Roll out some fondant and using a circle cutter or lid that's about the same size as the top of the cupcake cut out a disc. Place on top of the cupcake and smooth into place. Add further decoration if you wish.

BUTTERCREAM, WHITE ICING, AND FONDANT RECIPES

Buttercream

This is a simple uncomplicated recipe that produces buttercream suitable for both spreading and piping. The amounts given here are for what is referred to throughout the book as "1 quantity."

1 cup (8 oz / 250 g) butter (softened):
4 cups (1 lb / 450 g) confectioners' sugar:
1 teaspoon vanilla extract
1 tablespoon hot water

1 If you are using a mixer, place all the ingredients into a mixing bowl and bind them together on a slow speed. Then increase the speed and beat until the buttercream is pale and creamy.
2 If you are making it by hand, make sure the butter is very soft. Place all the ingredients into a large bowl and mix until smooth.
3 Unused or pre-prepared buttercream can be kept in a covered container in the refrigerator for up to a week or frozen for up to a month.

Flavoring and Coloring

There are many ways to flavor buttercream. Here are just a few suggestions.

Chocolate

1 Melt 3 1/2 ounces (100 g) of semi-sweet (plain) chocolate and stir into 1 quantity of buttercream.
2 Alternatively mix 1 tablespoon of cocoa powder into a paste with 1-2 tablespoons of hot water and stir into the buttercream.
3 You can increase these amounts if you prefer a stronger chocolate taste.

Coffee

Mix a tablespoon of instant coffee and a tablespoon of hot water together and stir into the buttercream.

Coloring Buttercream

Chocolate, coffee, and jam will automatically color the buttercream. You can also use food colors to create a frosting that is bright and vibrant. I would suggest using paste or gel colors as these are thicker and more concentrated than liquid colors so you'll use less and it won't make your buttercream runny.

Something Fruity

1 Stir a couple of tablespoons of jam into the buttercream to add both color as well as taste.
2 You can also buy commercial flavorings—peppermint, almond, lemon, and orange for example. Just add a few drops and mix in. Some are more concentrated than others so repeat until you're happy with the taste and strength.

White Royal Icing

This is made by mixing egg white with confectioners' sugar. It's a versatile white icing that sets very hard and brittle. It is excellent for piping fine details on cakes but should not be used as a cupcake topping. It cannot be used directly on sponge cakes.

I am including royal icing for anyone using a fruitcake base for cakes such as "Sledding Santa Cake." The fruitcake is first covered with almond paste (marzipan) then the royal icing is spread over the marzipan. This was the traditional way to cover a celebration cake in the UK for years until sponge and fondant became popular.

I use dried egg white to make my royal icing but you can use fresh eggs if you prefer.

You can omit the glycerine and lemon juice if you wish but these soften the icing to allow you to cut it fairly easily without it putting up too much resistance. You have been warned!

4 cups (500 g) confectioners' sugar
1 tablespoon or two 8 g sachets of dried egg white powder (meringue powder) or 4 egg whites
6 tablespoons of water—ONLY IF YOU ARE USING THE DRIED EGG WHITE
2 teaspoons glycerine
3 teaspoons lemon juice

1 If using dried egg white, place this and the confectioners' sugar in a clean grease free bowl. Stir together. Add the water, glycerine, and lemon juice. Bind the mixture together slowly. Add a tiny bit more water if it is becoming too lumpy. Leave the mixture on a slow speed for about five minutes until the mixture is thick, soft, and glossy and standing up in peaks.
2 If using real egg, beat the the egg whites until they become frothy . Add the sugar, lemon juice and glycerine and beat it for about 5 minutes on a slow speed until the mixture stands up in peaks.
3 If you need to add more water or sugar because your icing is too hard or too runny, do so gradually by adding tiny amounts.
4 Royal icing will start to harden as soon as it comes into contact with air so put it into an airtight plastic container until you are ready to use it. Scrape it into the container, and place a strip of plastic wrap directly on the top to keep air out. Place the lid on the container.

PREPARING THE FRUITCAKE

Before you cover your fruitcake with fondant or royal icing you will need to cover it with almond paste (marzipan) first. This is to stop the oils from the cake seeping though the icing.

Soft White Icing

For some cakes, buttercream just isn't white enough—if you're making a snow scene for example. Substitute white vegetable fat for butter and the problem's solved. I found I could buy white vegetable fat that contained no hydrogenated vegetable oil, no "e" numbers and no colors or preservatives. After all, butter is a fat too and we're quite happy eating that.

1 cup (8 oz/250 g) white vegetable fat
4 cups (1 lb /450 g) confectioners' sugar
2 teaspoons vanilla extract
2 tablespoons hot water

Place all the ingredients into a bowl. Gently bind together then beat until smooth.

Fondant

There are quite a lot of different names for rolled fondant icing including sugarpaste and ready-to-roll icing. It is sold in supermarkets and cake decorating shops and can also be ordered over the Internet. It has grown in popularity over the past ten years or so because it is extremely easy to use. I buy mine ready made but you can make it from scratch if you prefer.

4 cups (1 lb /500 g) confectioners' sugar
1 egg white or equivalent dried egg white
  (meringue powder) reconstituted
2 tablespoons corn syrup (liquid glucose)

1 Sieve the sugar into a large bowl and make a well in the center.
2 Pour the egg white and corn syrup into the well and stir in. Use your hands or the bread kneading attachment on your mixer if it has one to knead the fondant together. Knead until it becomes silky and smooth.
3 Double wrap the fondant in two plastic food bags to prevent it from drying out. It can be used immediately. It does not have to be refrigerated but should be used within a week.

Method

1 If your design requires a level cake but yours looks a bit domed, slice a little off the top and turn the fruitcake upside down and place it onto the cake board. If there is a gap between the board and the cake, press a little marzipan into it. If you wish, pierce the top a few times with a toothpick and drizzle a little brandy over the top. Fill any holes with little bits of marzipan.

2 You will need some jam (apricot is ideal as it has a very mild taste) to stick the almond paste (marzipan) to the fruitcake. Place a couple of tablespoons of jam into a heatproof bowl and microwave for a couple of minutes until it is boiling. Carefully remove the bowl and using a pastry brush paint the jam over the sides and top.
3 Dust your work surface with confectioners' sugar and knead and roll out the almond paste (marzipan). If it's hard you can soften it with a quick blast in the microwave. Don't overdo it though as the oil in the marzipan can get very hot and could burn.
4 Lift and place the marzipan over the cake. Smooth the top and sides into place. Again use a cake smoother if you have one for a really neat finish. Trim any excess from around the base.
5 If you're covering the cake with fondant, dab some cooled boiled water over the marzipan to make it sticky. Roll

out the fondant as described above and cover the cake.
6 If you are covering the cake with royal icing, ideally allow the marzipan to dry out for a day or so. Do not wet the marzipan before spreading royal icing over it.

PREPARING A SPONGE CAKE

Once your cake is baked and cooled you are ready for the exciting part!
But first there are a few necessary steps to prepare your cake.

Fig. 1

Fig. 2

Fig. 3

Fig. 4

Fig. 5

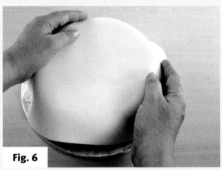
Fig. 6

Preparing Your Sponge Cake

Many of the cake designs require you to "level your cake." To get the top of your cake flat and level is easy – just turn it upside down. Let me explain.

When your cake comes out of the oven the top has usually risen into a dome shape. Slice this off (Fig. 1) and turn the cake upside down. What was once the base should now become a nice flat top (Fig. 2).

Slice Your Cake Into layers

Next you need to slice your cake into two or three layers. Before you do though, make a vertical buttercream mark on the side of the cake. This will help you replace the layers back in the same position. Slice the cake into layers. Dab each layer with stock syrup if you wish and spread jam or buttercream over the top. Reassemble the cake lining up the buttercream marks (Fig.3).

Coat Your Cake

You can coat the cake with either jam or buttercream. This will act as a "glue" to hold the fon-

dant covering in place. Using a spatula spread buttercream around the sides of the cake. If you do the sides first you can hold the top steady with your free hand. Then coat the top. (Fig. 4) The buttercream needs to be tacky so that it can grip the fondant so to stop it drying out place some plastic wrap over the buttercreamed cake until you're ready with the fondant (Fig. 5).

Covering Your Cake

The fondant for covering the cake needs to be soft and pliable so either knead it for a few minutes on a surface dusted with confectioners' sugar to prevent sticking or microwave it for 15-20 seconds.

Dust your work surface with a little confectioners' sugar and roll the fondant out using a rolling pin. If you find the sugar too dusty you can smear a little white fat over your work surface instead but be sparing or everything will become very greasy. Roll the fondant out to a thickness of about 1/4 inch (5 mm). Slide a knife under the fondant if you wish to ensure it's not stuck to your work surface.

To place the fondant onto the cake slide your

Fig. 7

hands palms uppermost underneath the fondant lift and place onto the cake.(Fig. 6) Alternatively, roll it loosely around your rolling pin like you would pastry then hold it over the sponge and allow it to fall gently over the cake.

Smooth the fondant into place. Start with the top to prevent air getting trapped and forming a bubble, then ease the fondant down the sides.

You can use your hands to do all this but a pair of cake smoothers will give your cakes a really smooth finish. Use them to iron out any lumps and bumps (Fig. 7).

Finally, trim away any excess from around the base.

WORKING WITH FONDANT

Fondant is easy to use. You can create models, press shapes into it, roll it, stretch it, and even frill it. But there are a few basic rules that will help you create successful cakes.

1 Always keep unused fondant tightly wrapped in plastic food bags as it will dry out when exposed to air.

2 Have a bowl of water and a bowl of confectioners' sugar nearby. The water is for sticking the models together and the sugar is to prevent your fingers from getting sticky.

3 Avoid the temptation to remove icing sugar marks until your model is complete. Then brush away dusty marks using a soft damp paintbrush. The fondant will go shiny initially but will revert to its original matte finish.

4 Wipe off any water drips immediately or they will start to dissolve the fondant and leave you with a drip-sized hollow.

5 Make up the colors you know you will be using before you start.

6 Use paste or gel colors as liquid colors can make the fondant soggy and unuseable.

7 Although some of the step shots show exploded figures they are intended as a guide. Don't make all the components before you start or bits will start to dry out. Make up the sections as you go.

> **PROBLEMS:** *If you discover you have an air bubble trapped under the fondant prick it with a dressmaker's pin held at a slight angle and gently press the air out. If it still looks odd, pop a flower or something over the top.*
>
> *Cracking on the edge of the cake is a common problem. It's usually because the fondant is slightly dry. It will probably only be you who sees them, but if you're really concerned, try rubbing a tiny amount of white fat over the cracks. This can sometimes seal them. Alternatively, rub a little icing sugar over them and fill them that way. If all else fails hide them under a bit of decoration.*

COLORING FONDANT

1 Commercially made ready colored fondant is available in a whole spectrum of shades. It is also easy to color your own. To do this use food color pastes or gels. These are thicker than liquid colors so you won't need to use as much and it won't make the fondant soggy.

2 Use a fresh toothpick (cocktail stick), which you can throw away afterwards to apply the color. Yes, I know it's tempting to stick your paintbrush or craft knife straight into the pot but you risk contaminating the entire lot. Knead the color in adding more if you need to.

3 You can also knead different colored lumps of fondant together. For example, white and a little bit of red fondant will make pink; red and yellow will make orange. When you begin kneading, the fondant will initially look streaky. Roll it out at this point and you will get a marbled effect, which is what I used on A Christmas Skating Cake (page 62). Continue kneading to make the fondant a solid color.

CREATING FLESH TONES

1 You can create pinkish flesh tones easily using food color pastes in shades of "paprika" or "chestnut." Alternatively, mix a little pink, yellow, and white fondant together.

2 For darker skin tones, use brown food color paste or knead some black, red, and green fondant together. Add more white if you want to lighten the resulting color.

COLORING SUGAR AND COCONUT

1 You can color sugar or desiccated coconut easily. Tip a little sugar or coconut into a bowl. Add some food coloring and mix it together. I find doing this by hand is easiest. If you're concerned about staining, wear a disposable plastic glove.

2 Green colored sugar or coconut makes great grass. Mix a little black in and it looks like gravel. Incidentally if ever you're asked to make a beach or a garden, light brown sugar makes excellent sand and dark brown sugar makes good soil.

COVERING THE CAKE BOARD

All-In-One Method

This is an easy way of covering a board. The hardest part is lifting the cake onto it afterwards without marking the cake! Moisten the cake board with water. Knead your fondant until soft and begin to roll it out on your work surface. Lift and place the partially rolled out fondant onto the board and continue rolling up to and over the edges of the board. Run over the surface with a cake smoother if you have one and trim any excess away from the edges.

The Bandage Method

When the iced cake is in position, lightly moisten the visible cake board with a little water. Roll out and cut out a long strip of fondant that is wider than the exposed board and long enough to go round the cake. Cut a thin strip off one long edge to neaten it and slide your knife under the fondant to ensure it's not stuck to your work surface. Roll the fondant up like a loose bandage and, with the flat cut edge up against the cake, unwind it around the board. Neaten the join and edges.

The Fabric Method

Your iced cake should be in place. Moisten the board with water and roll out your fondant. Lift a section of fondant and place it up against the cake. Drape it over the board allowing it to fall into folds as you go. It may take three or four sections to cover the entire board. Neaten the edges.

The Sweet Way

Because sometimes you just don't have the time. Scatter a few sweets or candies around the board and no child at the party will notice a bit of exposed cake board!

CAKE DOWELS

1 To stop heavy decorations such as the baby's pram sinking into the cake there is a hidden cake dowel inside the cake that bears the weight.
2 Push the dowel (a food safe plastic rod) vertically into the cake until it reaches the base cake board. Make a mark with a pencil or a food color pen where the rod is level with the top of the cake.
3 Remove the dowel and make a partial cut with a serrated knife where the mark is located. Snap the dowel and place the now shorter length back into the cake. The top of it should be level with the top of the cake. You can now place the decoration on top with no fear of it sinking.

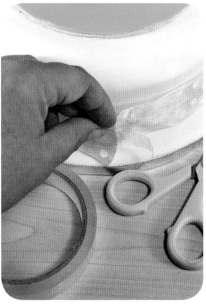

CANDY CANE REINDEER

1 I can't claim credit for this idea. My son's teacher made them for all her pupils last Christmas. However I thought it would be such a lovely addition to a seasonal party bag it was worth passing on.
2 Wind a pipe cleaner around the curve of the candy cane and bend into antlers. Use a little red pom pom for the nose and stick in place with a tiny bit of double sided sticky tape. Thank you, Miss Hankin!

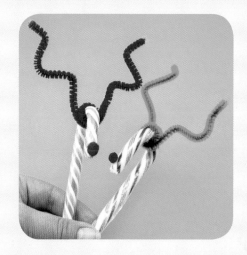

RIBBONS

Ribbons are a very quick and easy way to bring color to your cake design. Stand it around the side of the cake and secure at the back with a little sticky tape. The tape should not touch the cake itself and the join should be at the back.

Ribbons Round Board Edges
You will notice that most of the cakes have ribbons around the edges of the boards. It's not essential that you do this but if you want to use either small sections of double sided sticky tape or a non-toxic glue stick to keep the ribbon in place. Make sure the join is at the rear of the cake and if using the glue stick, try it out on a small section of ribbon first to ensure that it does not bleed through the ribbon.

A CHRISTENING CAKE

This naughty little scamp has not only pulled the fondant off the cake but also wrapped himself in it. To make the exposed cake look neater I baked the cake in two 7-inch (18 cm) shallow cake pans. It's not essential and you could bake the cake in a deeper pan and simply slice it in half or thirds as usual. If you are having a large party you could bake a second larger cake and use this one as the top tier or place the cake in the center of a large plate or board and surround it with cupcakes.

Ingredients
Two 7 in (18 cm) cakes baked in shallow
    cake pans (sandwich pans)
10 in (25 cm) round cake board or plate
5-6 tablespoons of jelly (jam)
1 quantity buttercream (see page 24)
4 oz (120 g) flesh-colored fondant
1 lb 2 oz (500 g) white fondant

1/8 oz (5 g) Yellow fondant
Black food coloring
1 strand raw, uncooked spaghetti
    (optional)
Confectioners' sugar for rolling out
    fondant on
Water, boiled and cooled for sticking
    fondant together

Equipment
10 in (25 cm) round cake board or plate
Small, sharp, non-serrated knife
Fine and medium paintbrushes
Metal piping tip (nozzle) any design
Cheeky straw (see page 11)
Scalpel (optional)
Rolling pin
Carving knife
Palette knife

TIPS: *No scalpel? Paint eyelashes instead with black food color or use a black food color pen once the fondant has hardened.*

For a neat blanket edge, place a large dinner plate on top of the rolled out fondant, then use it as a template to cut out a large disc.

How to Make Your Christening Cake

1 Begin by making the baby. Roll about 1 1/2 ounces (45 g) of flesh-colored fondant into an oval for the body (Fig. 1). Insert a section of spaghetti to add extra support if you wish. Leave about 3/4 inch (2 cm) protruding. Make a 1 ounce (30 g) flesh-colored ball for the head and stick on top of the body.

2 Holding it at an angle, press the edge of the piping tip into the face to make a smile. Press a little "U" shape with the cheeky straw at either edge of the mouth. Make and stick two tiny white fondant ball shapes onto the face for the eyes. Make the eyelashes by pressing the tip of the scalpel into the fondant three times at the outer edge of each eye (Fig. 2).

3 Add a tiny flesh-colored ball shape for the nose and some thin yellow fondant string shapes for hair. Paint pupils onto the eyes with black food color.

4 Make a small flat oval shape for the hand and stick over the mouth. Roll the remaining flesh-colored fondant (about 1 ounce / 30 g) into a sausage about 5 inches (13 cm) long. Cut it in half and, with the rounded ends forming the feet, bend each half into an "L" shape. Stick the legs against the body.

5 Place a layer of jam (jelly) and buttercream over the top of the first cake and place the second layer on top. Sit the baby in position on the cake.

6 Knead the white fondant until pliable and roll into a ball. Using your rolling pin, flatten it into a large disc (see TIPS). Dab a little water on the baby's head then lift and place the white icing over the baby and most of the cake.

7 Tweak the white fondant into an attractive arrangement. Poke a pattern of dots around the edge of the white with the end of your paintbrush (Fig. 3).

Fig. 1

Fig. 2

Fig. 3

CHRISTENING CUPCAKES

Roll about 1/3 ounce (10 g) of flesh-colored fondant into an oval for the body. Stand upright and stick a 1/8 ounce (5 g) fondant ball on top for the head. Add two tiny white fondant ball shapes for eyes and press the edge of a piping nozzle (tip) held at an angle into the lower part of the face to make a smile. Add a tiny fondant ball for a nose and a tiny yellow fondant string bent into a squiggle for the hair. To make the blanket, thinly roll out about 2/3 ounce (20 g) of white fondant. Cut out a strip about 4 x 1 1/2 inches (10 x 4 cm) Fringe both ends and wrap around the body. Paint dots on the eyes to finish.

BABY'S FIRST BIRTHDAY CAKE

As I was putting the first version of this baby cake together it occurred to me that if the baby in question hadn't chewed the pram, there was a strong chance the parents might like to keep it. So on this, the second version, I put the model on a small thin cake card. This means the model can be removed easily from the cake and kept. You may find it useful to do this with other designs when the recipient may want to keep your decorations (see page 29).

Ingredients
8 in (20 cm) round cake
1 quantity of buttercream (see page 24)
Confectioners' sugar for rolling out fondant on
Water, boiled and cooled for sticking fondant
1 lb 12 oz (800 g) white fondant
2 oz (60 g) green fondant
10 oz (300 g) pale blue fondant
1¹/2 oz (45 g) black fondant
Tiny bit of yellow fondant

²/3 oz (20 g) pink fondant
1 oz (30 g) brown fondant
Black food coloring

Equipment
6 in (15cm) thin round cake card
10 in (25 cm) normal round cake board
Carving knife
Palette knife
Rolling pin
Cake smoothers (optional)
Small, sharp, non-serrated knife
Medium and fine paintbrushes
Circle cutters—1¹/4 in (3 cm) and
    ³/4 in (2 cm) See TIPS opposite
Piping nozzle (tip)—any design

Scalpel (optional)
Ribbons
Scissors
Sticky tape
Plastic cake dowel (optional)

BABY'S FIRST BIRTHDAY CUPCAKES

Make a teddy bear using the instructions given in the main cake. You can change the body color if you wish—pink or blue for example to match the cupcake cases. Pipe or spread a swirl of buttercream onto the top of your cake and place the teddy bear on top.

How to Make Your Baby's First Birthday Cake

1 Level the top of the cake and turn it upside down. Split and fill the center with buttercream. Reassemble the cake and place on the larger board. Coat the outside surfaces with buttercream and cover using about 1 pound 8 ounces (700 g) of white fondant. Smooth the top and sides. Trim and keep any excess from around the base.

2 Keep about 1/3 ounce (10 g) of white fondant back for the baby's bonnet. Moisten the exposed cake board and cover it using the rest of the white fondant. Use the bandage method shown on page 28. Then place the cake to one side.

3 Lightly moisten the small board with a little water. Knead the green fondant until pliable and roll it into a thick circle then place it on to the board. Continue to roll the fondant up to and over the edges of the board. Then trim off the excess and place to one side for the moment.

4 To make the pram, roll all the blue fondant into an oval about 3 inches (8 cm) long. Slice about a third off the length of the oval. The large section will form the body of the pram (Fig. 1).

5 Roll about 2/3 ounce (20 g) of blue fondant taken from the small cutaway piece into a thick oval about 1/3 inch (1 cm) thick. This will form a hidden support beneath the pram. Stick it onto the green board slightly to the left of center. Stick the body of the pram on top of the base. You should now have something that resembles a stumpy mushroom. Press tiny dots into the sides using the end of your paintbrush. (Fig. 2)

6 To make the wheels (See TIPS) roll the black fondant to a thickness of about 1/3 inch (1 cm). Using the largest cutter, cut out four discs. Press a circle inside each disc with the smaller cutter. Thinly roll out a little pale blue fondant and cut out four circles using the piping nozzle (tip). Stick one in the center of each wheel and press a dot into the center of each one with your paintbrush. Stick the wheels around the sides of the pram.

7 Thinly roll out about 1/3 ounce (10 g) of the pale blue fondant and cut out a rectangle about 3/4 x 2 1/2 inches (2 x 6 cm). Divide this into four equal rectangles and stick one over the top of each wheel.

8 Roll the all the leftover pale blue fondant (you should have about 1 1/2 ounces / 45 g) into a thick oval shape for the pram's hood. Stick it onto the back of the pram and press dots into the hood.

9 Take a 1/3 ounce (10 g) lump of flesh-colored fondant. Pull off about a quarter and roll both bits into oval shapes. Use the larger oval for the baby's body and stick it on top of the pram. The smaller bit will make his feet. Stick at the end of the larger oval standing upright.

10 Roll 1/2 ounce (15 g) of flesh-colored fondant into a thick disc shape for the head and stick it on top of the body. Add two tiny flattened white fondant balls for eyes and a tiny flesh-colored ball shaped nose.

11 Press a smile into his lower face using the edge of a piping nozzle (tip). Make three tiny cuts with the tip of a scalpel at the side of each eye for eyelashes. Alternatively, paint tiny food color lines or leave off completely.

12 Roll a tiny bit of yellow fondant into an "S" shape for the hair and stick onto the forehead. Thinly roll out about 1/8 ounce (5 g) of white fondant and cut out a rectangle about 3 x 1/3 inch (8 x 1 cm) for the baby's bonnet. Frill the edge by lightly rolling the end of your paintbrush backwards and forwards along one long edge (Fig. 3). Stick the frill around the baby's head.

13 For the blanket, thinly roll out the pink fondant and cut out a rectangle about 2 1/2 x 1 1/2 inches (6 x 4 cm). Press lines across the blanket with the back of your knife and cut a fringe into both of the shorter sides. Stick the blanket over the baby.

14 Roll a small bit of black fondant into a string about 3 inches (8 cm) long for the pram handle. Slice off the two rounded ends and stick in a loop shape at the rear of the pram. Use the blanket and feet for added support and allow the top of the loop to sag slightly.

15 To make the teddy bear, roll about 1/2 ounce (15 g) of brown fondant into an oval for his body. Stick a 1/8 ounce (5 g) ball of brown on top for his head. Stick a flat white fondant disc on his tummy and a small white fondant oval on his face. Press a line into the oval on his face with the back of your knife.

16 Make two tiny sausage shapes for his legs and bend the end of each one upwards slightly to make an "L" shape. Stick one on either side of the body and press four hollows into the base of each foot with the end of your paintbrush.

17 Make another two brown sausage shapes for arms and stick onto the body. Make two tiny ball shapes for ears and stick onto the head. Press a hollow into each ear with the paintbrush. Stick the teddy bear on the board next to the pram. Paint two black food color dots on the teddy bear's face and the pupils on the baby's eyes.

18 To finish, add some ribbon around the sides of the cake and the edges of the boards, too, if you wish, and scatter a few candies around the pram.

> **TIPS:** *The board should mean the weight of the model is spread evenly across the cake but if you're concerned the weight might press down too hard causing your cake to split (especially if you've been quite exuberant in your use of buttercream fillings) use a cake dowel. (See page 29)*
>
> *If you do not possess a circle cutter for making the wheels, keep a little bit of black fondant back for the handle. Divide the rest into four and roll into ball shapes. Flatten into four thick discs.*

Fig. 1

Fig. 2

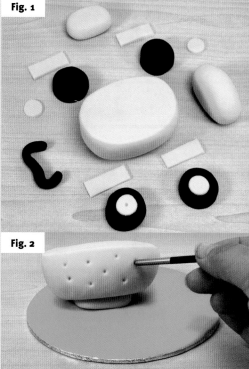

Fig. 3

HEY! IT'S A HOLIDAY CAKE!

This is a useful design that is quick to put together and that will work for a number of different occasions like holidays, "Welcome Home," anniversaries, etc. It would obviously work as a birthday cake too, but (here comes the health and safety announcement) keep candles well away from the edible wafer paper and flags. Remove the flags when cutting the cake; although they match the colors of the wafer paper, they are not edible.

Ingredients
8 in (20 cm) round cake
1 quantity buttercream (see page 24)
Confectioners' sugar for rolling out fondant on
Water, boiled and cooled for sticking
1 lb 6 oz (650 g) white fondant
6 oz (175 g) pink fondant
3-4 sheets of colored edible wafer paper (rice paper)
Candies for decoration

Equipment
10 in (25 cm) round cake board
Carving knife
Palette knife
Rolling pin
Cake smoother (optional)
Small, sharp, non-serrated knife
Paintbrush
27 in (69 cm) ribbon for cake
34 in (87 cm) ribbon for board (optional)
Scissors
Sticky tape
Hat templates (see pages 74 and 75)
Pencil
Non-toxic glue stick for sticking ribbon around board.
5 paper sandwich flags

TIPS: *It's really important not to get the wafer paper too wet or it will turn to mush. Keep a clean cloth or piece of kitchen paper nearby. Gently wipe your brush on it prior to sticking the wafer paper. This will remove any excess water*
If you can't find matching sandwich flags or would prefer edible flags, make your own by wrapping edible paper around toothpicks (cocktail sticks).

How to Make Your Hey! It's a Holiday Cake!

1 Slice a bit off the top of the cake to level it if necessary and turn it upside down. Split into layers and fill the center with buttercream. Reassemble the cake and place in the middle of the board. Coat the outside of the cake with buttercream.

2 Knead and roll out the white fondant. Lift and place it over the top of the cake. Smooth the top and sides and trim and neaten the base.

3 Lightly moisten the exposed cake board with a little water. Knead and roll the pink fondant into a long string. Flatten the string and cut out a long strip about 31 inches (79 cm) long and at least 1 inch (2.5 cm) wide.

4 Slide a knife under the length of the strip to ensure it's not stuck to your work surface and roll it up like a bandage. Unwind it around the base of the cake and cover the board. Smooth it into place and neaten the join and edges.

5 Stand ribbon around the base of the cake to hide the join between the cake and board and secure it at the back with a little sticky tape. Place the cake to one side.

6 To make a hat, place a piece of wafer paper over the hat template and trace over it with a pencil. Cut it out cutting just inside the pencil lines so that they won't be visible.

7 Fold the hat into a cone and paint a light line of water down one edge. Starting at the base, press the two ends together. (Fig. 1) Cut out a fringe in a contrasting color and stick on the top with a light dab of water. Make three hats.

8 To make the paper chains, you will need about 44 strips 3 x ¾ inch (8 x 2 cm). I had four different colors so made 11 of each color. Bend a strip into a circle and secure the join with a light dab of water. Thread the next chain through it and secure the join. (Fig. 2) Continue until all the strips are used up.

9 Make a little mark where each of the sandwich flags will stand. Thread the first chain onto one of the sandwich flags and stick the flag into the cake. Poke the next flag through the eighth chain and place in position. (Fig. 3) Continue around the cake so the chains hang neatly and evenly around the cake.

10 To finish, stand the hats in the center of the cake and scatter a few candies around the cake. Glue contrasting ribbons around the edge of the board, if you wish.

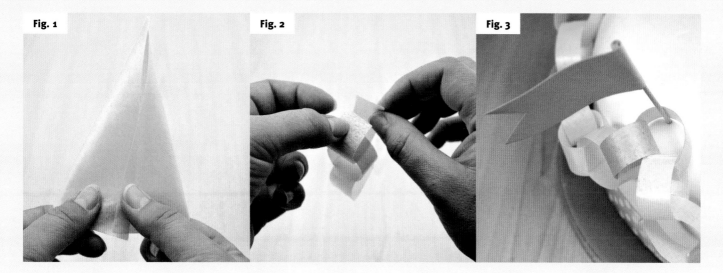

Fig. 1 **Fig. 2** **Fig. 3**

HOLIDAY CUPCAKES

To make the mini hats, cut out two edible wafer paper triangular shapes. (Template on page 75) Fold the paper to form a cone and stick the join together with a light dab of water. Cut out a triangle in a contrasting color for the tassel and stick on top with a little water. To make the curls, cut a thin strip of wafer paper, wind it around a pencil to make it curl. Remove the pencil and place onto the cupcake.

A NEW YEAR FIREWORKS CAKE

In this design a sneaky matchbox can be seen eyeing an understandably nervous firework. This cake would work for any event where fireworks are involved (Fourth of July, Bonfire Night). You could make a simpler rocket using two different colors of edible wafer paper. Follow the instructions for making a castle turret (page 77) but leave out the windows and draw a face on the front instead.

Ingredients

8 in (20 cm) round sponge cake
1 Baked Bean Can Cake (see page 14)
1 quantity buttercream (see page 24)
Confectioners' sugar for rolling out
   fondant on
Cooled, boiled water for sticking fondant
1 lb 8 oz (700 g) white fondant.
7 oz (200 g) green fondant
4 oz (120 g) yellow fondant
6 oz (175 g) red fondant
1/2 oz (15 g) black fondant
1 oz (30 g) blue fondant
1 breadstick
Black and green food color pastes
1 strand raw uncooked spaghetti

Equipment

10 in (25 cm) round cake board
Carving knife
Palette knife
Rolling pin
Cake smoothers (optional)
Small, sharp, non-serrated knife
Fine and medium paintbrushes

FIREWORK CUPCAKES

Slice a little off the top of the cupcake to level it and cover with a disc of dark blue fondant. Make a 1 ounce (30 g) yellow fondant sausage shape and cut off the two rounded ends. Make a small red fondant carrot shape and slice the rounded end off that. Stick the two together. Poke a short length of raw uncooked spaghetti into the base of the firework. Make two thin pale blue fondant strings and stick one around each end of the yellow section to neaten it. Place the firework onto the cupcake and add press a few edible gold balls into the dark blue "sky."

To Make Your New Year Fireworks Cake

Fig. 1

1 Level the cake and turn it upside down. Split and fill the center with buttercream. Reassemble the cake and place in the center of the board. Coat the top and sides with buttercream and cover with the white fondant. Smooth it into place and trim and neaten around the base. Keep a little bit back to use for the eyes later.

2 Knead and thinly roll out the green fondant. Cut out a long tapering triangular shape for a blade of grass. Paint a light line of water down the length of the blade and stick it up the side of the cake allowing the base to both cover the exposed cake board and overhang it a little. (Fig.1)

> **TIPS:** *Don't over fill the center of the cake with buttercream otherwise the weight of the firework cake sitting on the edge of the cake will squash that side of the cake down and possibly make it look a bit lop-sided. If you're concerned that this will happen cut a thin cake card down to size and place the firework on top. Support it from beneath with a cake dowel (see page 29)*
> *If you don't have a bake bean can shaped cake for the firework use a circle cutter or template to cut a small round cake out of a larger piece of cake. Alternatively, you could use a stack of cookies—anything that will produce the right cylindrical shape of a firework.*

3 Continue around the cake, scrunching up and re-rolling the fondant when necessary. The blades of grass do not need to be the same length. Keep the section where the firework stick will hang down shorter than the top of the cake. When done, run a knife around the edge of the board to neaten. Place the cake to one side.

4 Level the top of the Baked Bean Can Cake and turn it upside down. Coat the top and sides with buttercream and cover with the yellow fondant. Smooth the sides and trim around the base. Dust your work surface or a spare board with sugar to prevent the firework from sticking and carefully turn it the other way up so that the uncovered cake is now forming the top. Using the end of your paintbrush poke a little hollow into the base of the firework for his mouth (Fig. 2). Dab a little more buttercream onto the exposed cake.

5 Knead and shape 4 ounces (120 g) of red fondant into a rounded pointed shape for the top of the firework and stick it in place. Make two small white fondant ball shapes for the eyes, flatten them and stick them onto the front of the firework. Add two smaller black ovals and make a tiny yellow ball shape for a nose.

6 Dab a little water on the edge of the cake and carefully place the firework in position. It should overhang the edge of the cake a little but not too much or it will topple off. Cut a length of breadstick to length and carefully insert it into the base of the firework. You can also use a dab of buttercream to secure it against the side of the cake.

7 Paint a light line of water around the base of the firework's red top and the base of the firework itself. Knead and roll out about 1/2 ounce (15 g) of the blue fondant into a thin string about 12 inches (30 cm) long. Starting from the back, stick it around the base of the firework. Repeat around the base of the red top.

8 To make the matchbox, roll about 1 1/2 ounces (45 g) of red fondant to a thickness of about 1/3 inch (1 cm). Cut out a rectangle about 2 x 1 1/2 inches (5 x 4 cm) (Fig. 3). Press a line across the top of the box with the back of your knife and make sure it stands upright securely.

9 Make two tiny white fondant leaf shapes for his eyes and stick on the front of the box. Make two tiny red fondant "S" shapes for his eyebrows and stick them on top of his eyes.

Make a tiny carrot shape for his nose and stick in place. Paint black food color dots on the eyes and a mean smile on his face! While you have the black food color out, paint two eyebrows on the yellow firework.

10 Make a tiny black ball for the matchstick head and poke a short length of spaghetti into it. Make two tiny red fondant sausage shapes for his arms and stick against his sides. Poke the match behind his arm so it looks as though he's holding it. Stick the matchbox into position.

11 Dab a little watered down green food color around the top of the cake.

Fig. 2

Fig. 3

CHINESE DRAGON CAKE

The carving of the cake to make the dragon's body may seem daunting at first but once you have mastered it you can use the same shape to make snakes, caterpillars, alligators, or monster cakes—anything in that requires a bendy "S" shaped body (or inverted "S" shape). You could also use it to make a "S" shaped cake for someone who's name begins with "S." The dragon is also a great demonstration of how just how far you can stretch an eight-inch cake. You could easily feed 30 people with this monster. He sits on the largest board in the book so he would certainly make a fearsome impression at any party!

Ingredients
8 in (20 cm) round cake
2 sheets green colored edible wafer paper (rice paper)
2 sheets yellow colored edible wafer paper
1 sheet white edible wafer paper
3 quanties buttercream (see page 24)
Red food color paste
1 lb 2 oz (500 g) green fondant
10 oz (300 g) yellow fondant
3 oz (90 g) white fondant
1/2 oz (15 g) black fondant
Edible gold balls or small sweets to decorate board
Confectioners' sugar for rolling out fondant on
Water, boiled and cooled for sticking

Equipment
16 in (40 cm) round cake board
Dragon templates for tail, spikes, facial features—see pages 75-77
Pencil
Scissors
Rolling pin
Cake smoothers (optional)
Small, sharp, non-serrated knife
Spare cakeboard or chopping board for carving cake on
Carving knife
3 1/2 in (9 cm) circle cutter or template (page 78)
Spatula or fish slice
Palette knife
Large piping bag (see page 79)
Large star piping nozzle (tip)
Normal small metal piping nozzle (tip)—any design
Paintbrush

CHINESE DRAGON CUPCAKES

Cut out two white edible paper teeth (templates page 77), two sets of eyebrow shapes and two copies of the smaller side-whiskers. Make two white discs for eyes. Make three tiny black discs: two for the eyes and one for the nose. Pipe red stars over the top of the cupcake. Pipe some extra ones at the front to build up the front part of the face. Place the eyes, teeth and nose in position and arrange the other sections around the cupcake.

How to Make Your Chinese Dragon Cake

Fig. 1

1 Begin by cutting out all the edible wafer paper decorations (Fig. 1). You will need the two tail spikes, (one green, one yellow); 18 spikes for his back (9 in green, 9 in yellow), 2 large green facial spikes, 2 large yellow facial spikes, 4 smaller green face spikes and 4 smaller yellow facial spikes. Oh, and one set of white teeth! Place the paper over the relevant shape, trace the outline in pencil and cut out. Try to cut just inside the pencil lines so that they don't show. Place to one side for the moment.

2 To make the eyes, roll and flatten two ¹/₃ ounce (10 g) balls of white fondant. Make and stick two black fondant discs on top and finish with two tiny flat white discs. For the nose, roll ¹/₈ ounce (5 g) of black fondant into an oval shape and press two hollows into it with the end of your paintbrush.

3 Use 1¹/₂ ounces (45 g) of yellow fondant for each front leg. Roll the fondant into two thick carrot shapes and flatten slightly. Bend them both into a curve and using a metal piping nozzle held at an angle, press "U" shapes for scales into the legs. Repeat for the back legs except use about 3 ounces (90 g) of yellow fondant for each back leg.

4 Dab water over the cake board and knead and roll out the green fondant. Lift and place the fondant onto the board and continue rolling up to and over the edges. Smooth the fondant and trim and neaten the edges. Place the

Fig. 2

board to one side.

5 To cut the cake to shape, first level the top and turn it upside down. Cut a circle out of the middle about 3¹/₂ inches (9 cm) in diameter using a cutter or by cutting round the template. Then cut the cake in half. (Fig. 2)

6 Arrange the two big sections of cake into an

Fig. 3

inverted "S" shape on a cutting board (Fig. 3). You can now cut these cakes into layers and sandwich them together with buttercream. Carefully spread a light layer of buttercream over the top and sides and, if you can, place into the refrigerator for about 20 minutes so the buttercream can set and harden. This will make it less likely that you get crumbs onto the covered board when you place it onto it.

7 When ready, carefully lift and place the buttercreamed cake onto the covered board using a spatula. Make sure you leave enough room for the head later. Roll about 1¹/₂ ounces (45 g) of white fondant into a triangle and stick onto the tail end.

8 Color the remaining buttercream red and put some into the piping bag fitted with the star nozzle (tip). Close the bag and press the tip gently against the cake. Squeeze a little buttercream out, release the pressure and pull away leaving a tapering star behind. Once you have piped around the base, pipe another layer above. Continue until the dragon's body is covered.

9 Press the two tail sections into the tail and press a line of spikes along his back, alternating the green and yellow triangles.

10 To make the head, slice the leftover disc of cake in half as shown in Fig. 3, and buttercream together as shown. Coat the tops and sides then place in position against the dragon's body. Pipe over the head as before.

11 Place the eyes, and facial spikes in position—the larger spikes at the back of the head, the smaller sets as eyebrows and whiskers. Add the nose and teeth.

12 Place the legs in position and make some tiny white carrot shapes for claws and stick three of them onto the end of each leg.

13 To finish, pipe dots of buttercream onto the board and stick the edible gold balls in place.

> **TIPS:** *You could use a gold colored cake board instead of a normal silver one. The gold would look so ceremonial that you wouldn't have to cover it with fondant. Obviously this is a busy time of year so you could bake the cake and make up the buttercream in advance and freeze them. Also, have all the edible wafer paper sections, legs and eyes made up and stored ready for the big day.*

FATHER'S DAY GOLFER CAKE

Disaster! The ball stopped just short of the hole so dad's trying to blow it in! Okay so it's cheating but as it's Father's Day we'll let him get away with it this time! The golfer can be made well in advance and popped on top of the cake when needed.

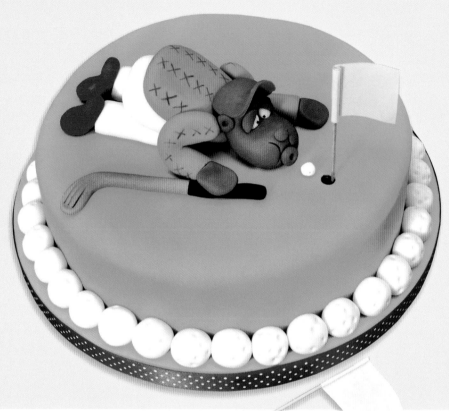

Ingredients

8 in (20 cm) round cake
1 quantity buttercream (see page 24)
Confectioners' sugar for rolling out fondant on
Water, boiled and cooled for sticking
1 lb 10 oz (750 g) green fondant
8½ oz (275 g) white fondant
2½ oz (75 g) blue fondant
1½ oz (45 g) flesh-colored fondant
⅔ oz (20 g) red fondant
½ oz (15 g) gray fondant
Black food color

Equipment

10 in (25 cm) round cake board
Carving knife
Palette knife
Rolling pin
Cake smoothers (optional)
Small, sharp, non-serrated knife
Paintbrushes—fine and medium
Piping nozzle (tip) any design
1½ in (4 cm) circle cutter or lid (optional—see step 9)
Toothpick (cocktail stick)
Small paper sandwich flag
Scissors

FATHER'S DAY GOLF BAG CUPCAKES

Level the top of the cupcake and cover with a disc of green fondant. Roll about 1 ounce (30 g) of red fondant into a sausage shape. Flatten slightly and poke a little hollow into the top with the end of your paintbrush for the golf clubs later. Thinly roll out a little red fondant and cut out a square for the pocket and stick it on top of the bag. Press a line across the pocket with the back of your knife and use the point of a piping tip (nozzle) to make a tiny button impression. Cut a thin strip for the strap and stick across the bag. Make two tiny gray fondant "L" shapes for the clubs. Press a couple of lines into the head of both clubs and stick into the top of the bag. Place onto the cupcake and stick a tiny white fondant golf ball by the side of the bag.

How to Make Your Father's Day Golfer Cake

1 Level the top of the cake and turn it upside down. Split and fill the middle of the cake with buttercream. Reassemble the cake and place it on the board. Apply buttercream to the sides and top.

2 Knead 1 pound 6 ounces (600 g) of green fondant until pliable. Roll it out and lift and place over the cake. Smooth the top and sides and trim and neaten the base.

3 Lightly moisten the exposed board around the base of the cake with a little water. Using 5 ounces (150 g) of green fondant, cover the board using the bandage method shown on page 28.

4 To make your golfer, begin with his legs. Roll 2 ounces (60 g) of white fondant into a sausage about 8 inches (20 cm) long (Fig. 1). Bend the sausage into a "U" shape then lift the rounded end and fold it back on itself (Fig. 2).

5 Roll 2 ounces (60 g) of blue fondant into an oval shape for his torso. Flatten slightly and stick with a dab of water on top of the legs. It should lie at an angle with the front end resting on the surface of the cake.

6 Roll 1 ounce (30 g) of flesh-colored fondant into an oval for his face. Slightly flatten the top half of the face and stick in position so that the thickest part of the oval rests on the cake and forms his chin.

7 Holding a piping nozzle at an angle, press two semi-circle indentations into the lower part of his face to form his cheeks (Fig. 3). To make the mouth, stick a tiny flesh-colored ball between his cheeks then poke a hollow into it using the end of a paintbrush.

8 Make two tiny white fondant balls for his eyes and then flatten them. Stick them onto the face. Make a third flesh-colored ball for his eyelids. Flatten it and cut in half. Stick one half at an angle over each eye. Make a tiny flesh-colored ball for his nose and stick in position.

9 To make his cap, thinly roll out about 1/3 ounce (10 g) of red fondant. Cut out a disc about 1 1/2 inches (4 cm) in diameter using a circle cutter or lid (If you have neither, make a ball and squash it) Stick the disc on top of the head and tweak the brim upwards.

10 While you have the red out, make two 1/8 ounce (5 g) red oval shapes for his shoes and stick one on the end of each leg.

11 Make two tiny flesh-colored ball shapes for his ears and stick one either side of his head. Poke the end of a paintbrush into each ear.

12 Make his arms by rolling about 1/2 ounce (15 g) of blue fondant into a sausage about 4 inches (10 cm) long. Cut the sausage in half and stick one either side of his body. The rounded ends should form his shoulders.

13 Roll 1/2 ounce (15 g) gray fondant into a long string about 4 inches (10 cm) long for the golf club. Bend and squash one end to form the "L" shaped golf club head and press three lines into it using the back of your knife. Lay and stick the golf club on the cake next to your golfer.

14 Using a fine paintbrush and some black food color, paint the top third of the golf club black. Paint black food color dots on the eyes.

15 Make two small flesh-colored ball shapes for his hands and flatten slightly. Stick one at

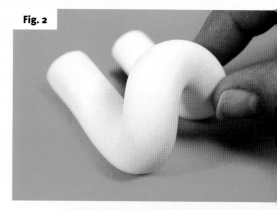

Fig. 2

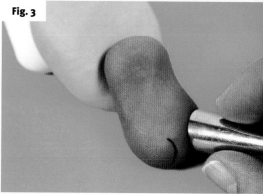

Fig. 3

the end of each arm with one resting on the top of the golf club.

16 Using the end of your paintbrush, poke a shallow hollow into the top of the cake in front of the golfer. If you dab a little black food color inside the "hole" it will give the impression of seeming much deeper than it actually is.

17 Make a tiny white fondant ball and stick onto the cake between the golfer's mouth and the hole. All three should line up. Poke some tiny holes into the ball using the end of a toothpick (cocktail stick).

18 Stand a sandwich flag inside the hole.

19 Make about 36 white fondant ball shapes about 1/8 ounce (5 g) each in weight. Stick around the base of the cake and poke a few hollows into each one with the end of a paint-brush.

> **TIPS:** *If you're making this cake for a birthday, make a few extra golf balls and use them as candleholders. Keep them away from the flag.*
> *Add hair, a less pronounced chin and perhaps brighter colored clothes to turn him into a lady golfer.*

Fig. 1

MOTHER'S DAY CAKE

A chair is a valuable cake shape to be able to create because it is so useful. You can sit a man on it for Father's day or Santa Claus or a large snowman for Christmas, even a firework for a really unusual New Year's cake. Just a plain chair would also make the ideal birthday cake for an upholsterer!

Ingredients

7 in (18 cm) round cake
1 quantity buttercream (page 24)
Confectioners' sugar for rolling out fondant on
Cooled, boiled water for sticking fondant
1/2 oz (15 g) black fondant
2 lb (900 g) pink fondant
1 oz (30 g) brown fondant
1 lb (450 g) blue fondant
5 oz (150 g) flesh-colored fondant
5 oz (150 g) white fondant
Black food color paste
Chocolates to decorate

Equipment

12 in (30 cm) round cake board
Rolling pin
Small, sharp, non-serrated knife
Fine and medium paintbrushes
Carving knife
Palette knife
Cake smoothers (optional)
Flower cutter (optional, see step 6)
Piping nozzle (tip) (any design)
Cheeky straw (see page 11)

MOTHER'S DAY CHOCOLATE CUPCAKES

This may look like cheating as the decoration doesn't include any modelling but I've included it because sometimes you just need a simple, easy idea that won't cause too much stress. Pipe or spread buttercream on the top of your cupcake and plonk a chocolate on top. Easy!

> **TIPS:** *A metal spatula (fish slice) is useful for lifting the cake onto the board and avoiding fingermarks.*
> *If you're artistic you could paint a food color pattern on to the chair or stick cut out fondant shapes on instead.*

1 Start by making the miniature chocolate box so it has time to harden a little. This will make it less likely to lose its shape when you place it in position. Roll out the black fondant to a thickness of about 1/3 inch (1 cm) (Fig. 1). Cut out a rectangle about 1 1/4 x 1 inch (3 x 2.5 cm). Lay it flat and paint a little water around all four sides.

2 Roll about 1/3 ounce (10 g) of pink fondant into a long sausage shape. Flatten it and cut out a strip slightly wider than the height of the black rectangle and about 4 1/2 inches (11.5 cm) long. Stick it around

Fig. 1

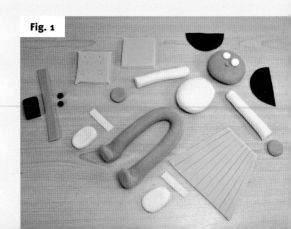

How to Make Your Mother's Day Cake

of each other. Using the cutter or template, cut a disc out of the top layer only. (Fig. 2) Remove and keep the disc. The remaining cake should now look like a chair shape but with pointed arms. Slice a little off the end of each arm to neaten. Fill the middle of the cake with buttercream. Assemble the chair and coat the outside of the cake with buttercream.

5 Knead and roll out about 1 pound 6 ounces (650 g) of the pink fondant and cover the chair. Make a small cut in the shape of a cross in the seat area (Fig. 3), so air won't get trapped. The cut will be hidden by the figure. Smooth it into place and trim and neaten the base.

6 Carefully lift and place the cake into position towards the rear of the covered board. Decorate your chair by pressing a cutter into the icing but be careful not to go all the way through. You could use any shape cutter or just the tip of your paintbrush to press spots into the fondant.

7 Paint a light line of water around the base of the chair. Roll about 2 ounces (60 g) of pink fondant into a long string about 21 inches (53 cm) long and lay and stick around the base of the chair. Press lines into it using the back of your knife.

8 Coat the outside of the small round section of cake and cover using about 5 ounces (150 g) of pink fondant. Trim and neaten the base and place onto the board to form a leg rest. Decorate to match the chair then roll about 1 ounce (30 g) of pink fondant into a thin string and stick around the base as before.

9 Make the cushions by rolling out about 3 ounces (90 g) of blue fondant out to a thickness of about 1/3 inch (1 cm). Cut out a rectangle about 2 1/2 x 2 inch (6 x 5 cm). Re-roll the leftover fondant to make a second cushion. Press four tiny circles for buttons into each cushion using the normal round end of the drinking straw. Press two or three tiny cuts radiating out from each button with the tip of your knife. Pinch each corner to form a point and stick both cushions at an angle on the rear of the seat.

10 To make mom, start with her legs. Roll about 2 1/2 ounces (75 g) of flesh-colored fondant into a sausage shape about 12 inches (30 cm) long. Bend it into a "U" shape and tweak the two ends upwards to form the feet. Stick the legs on the chair with the feet on the leg rest.

11 Roll 2 1/2 ounces (75 g) of white fondant into an oval shape for her body and stick on top of the legs resting against the cushions. Roll 1 1/2 ounces (45 g) of flesh-colored fondant into a ball for her head and stick on top of the body. She should look as though she's relaxing into the cushions. If her head starts to loll too far back so she begins to look as though she's undergone some sort of nasty accident, support it from behind with a ball of fondant.

12 Make two tiny white fondant ball shapes for her eyes. Flatten them and stick them onto her face. Using a piping nozzle, press a lop-sided smile onto her face. Press a tiny "U" shaped cheek on the end of the mouth using the cheeky straw and add a tiny fondant ball-shaped nose.

13 Thinly roll out 2/3 ounce (20 g) of brown fondant for her hair. Press lines across it with the back of your knife. Using the circle cutter or template, cut out a disc. Cut the disc in half and, with the straight edges at the back, stick her hair in place. Paint two black food color dots on her eyes.

14 Dab a little water on her legs and tummy then thinly roll out about 2 ounces (60 g) of blue fondant for her skirt. Cut out the skirt shape using the template if you wish although feel free to shorten the hem if your mother prefers a shorter skirt! Press lines down its length with the back of your knife. Drape and stick the skirt over the legs.

15 Roll about 1 ounce (30 g) of white fondant into a sausage about 6 inches (15 cm) long for her arms. Cut it in half. Make two flattish flesh-colored discs for her hands. Place the chocolate box in her lap and stick one arm and hand on as though she is holding the box.

16 Stick the spare chocolate on her chin and the second hand on top of it with the chocolate protruding. Bend the second arm at the elbow and stick in place between the shoulder and hand.

17 To make the slippers, thinly roll out about 1/3 ounce (10 g) of white fondant and cut out two thin strips about 1/3 inch (1 cm) wide. Stick one over the top of each foot. Divide about 1/8 ounce (5 g) of white fondant in half and roll into two oval shapes. Squash them both and stick onto the soles of her feet.

18 To finish, stick a few chocolates around the board and secure with light dabs of buttercream.

the black to form the sides of the box. Make some tiny brown fondant ball shapes for the chocolates and stick all but one into the top of the box. Press a couple of tiny cuts into the top of each chocolate with the tip of your knife. Place to one side.

3 Moisten the whole of the cake board with water and cover using about 10 ounces (300 g) of blue fondant. Use the all in one method shown on page 28. Place to one side to harden.

4 Level the cake and turn it upside down. Slice it in half horizontally but leave the two slices on top

Fig. 2

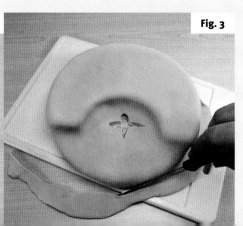

Fig. 3

VALENTINE CHERUB CAKE

Lose the arrows and take the wings off these cheeky cherubs and they become bouncing babies and the cake becomes a design suitable for a baby's shower or birthday party.

Ingredients

7 in (18 cm) round sponge cake
1 quantity buttercream (see page 24)
Confectioners' sugar for rolling out fondant on
Water, boiled and cooled for sticking fondant
8 oz (250 g) red fondant
1 lb 6 oz (650 g) white fondant
7 oz (200 g) pink flesh-colored fondant
2 oz (60 g) brown flesh-colored fondant
1/3 oz (10 g) yellow fondant
1/8 oz (5 g) black fondant
1 sheet edible wafer paper

Equipment

10 in (25 cm) round cake board
Carving knife
Palette knife
Paintbrushes – medium & fine
Rolling pin
Cake smoothers (optional)
Small, sharp, non-serrated knife
Spatula (fish slice)
Wing template (page 78)
24 in (61 cm) ribbon
Scissors
Sticky tape
3 toothpicks (cocktail sticks)

VALENTINE CHERUB CUPCAKES

Use the same instructions for making the central sitting cherub on the main cake. Once he's made, pipe an extravagant swirl of buttercream onto your cupcake place him lovingly on top. Place him into a box or put him on a pretty plate and and present to your beloved!

How to Make Your Valentine Cherub Cake

Fig. 1   Fig. 2   Fig. 3

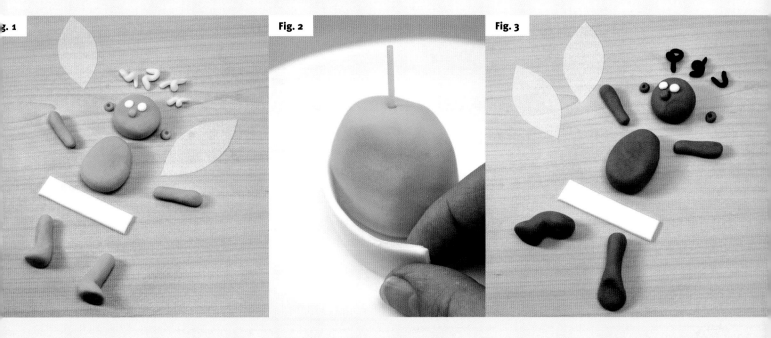

1 Lightly moisten the entire cake board with water. Knead and roll out the red fondant. Place the fondant on to the cake board and continue rolling until the board is covered. Trim and neaten the edges and place to one side.

2 Level the cake and turn it over. Split and fill with buttercream. Reassemble the cake and spread buttercream around the top and sides.

3 Knead and roll out 1 pound 6 ounces (600 g) of white fondant. Lift and cover the cake. Smooth the top and sides and trim and neaten the base.

4 Using a spatula, carefully lift and place the cake into position on the board. Place ribbon around the base and secure at the back with a little sticky tape.

5 To make the sitting cherub, roll 1 1/2 ounces (45 g) of flesh-colored fondant into an oval shape for his body (Fig. 1). Stick him upright with a light dab of water on the center of the cake.

6 Roll 1/8 ounce (5 g) of white fondant into a thin strip and starting from the back, stick it around the base of his body (Fig. 2).

7 Roll 1/2 ounce (15 g) of flesh-colored fondant into a sausage about 3 1/2 inches (9 cm) long for his legs. Cut the sausage in half. Bend one rounded end up slightly to form an "L" shape for his foot and stick in position against his body. Repeat with the other leg.

8 Make a 1-ounce (30 g) flesh-colored ball shape for his head and stick on top of his body.

9 Make two tiny white fondant ball shapes for eyes. Flatten them and stick them onto the face. Make two tiny flesh-colored ball shapes for ears and stick one to either side of his head. Poke the end of a paintbrush into each ear to leave a round imprint. Make a third tiny flesh-colored ball for his nose and stick in position.

10 To make the arrow, cut out a tiny wafer paper triangle and thread onto the tip of toothpick. Make another two.

11 Roll 1/8 ounce (5 g) of flesh-colored fondant into a sausage about 2 inches (5 cm) long for his arms. Cut the sausage in half and with the rounded ends forming his hands, stick the arms in place. Place one of the arrows into his arms.

12 Roll a little yellow fondant into a thin string and twist it into a curl. Stick on top of his head. Repeat with three more yellow fondant strings.

13 Paint two black food color dots on his eyes and a smile on his face.

14 Cut two wing shapes out of the wafer paper and carefully insert into his back. Or stick with a light dab of water.

15 Make another cherub to sit on the board in exactly the same way except he will only need one ear and position his arms so they cover his mouth.

16 For the climbing cherub make a 1-ounce (30 g) brown fondant oval for his body (Fig. 3) and stick on the edge of the cake. Roll 1/8 ounce (5 g) of brown fondant into a sausage for his arms. Cut in half and stick so they rest on the cake.

17 Make a 1/3-ounce (10 g) fondant ball for his head and stick on top of the arms. Add two eyes, ears, nose, and hair as before.

18 Roll 1/2 ounce (15 g) of brown fondant into a sausage for his legs. Cut in half. Stick one as though hanging down the side of the cake. Bend the other at the knee and stick with the foot on top of the cake.

19 Cut out two wings and insert or stick onto his back.

> **TIPS:** If it would help, you can cover the board a few days before you make the cake.
>
> If you make a few unsightly fingermarks lifting the cake, make a few icing hearts and stick them over the top.
>
> If you don't want to use toothpicks (cocktail sticks) for the arrows use raw dried spaghetti instead.

VALENTINE HEART CAKE

To help give them support, the hearts are actually cookies as fondant on its own just wouldn't be strong enough. If you don't like the idea of the cookies, leave them out. Cut two large hearts out of pink fondant and lay them flat on the top of the cake instead. You can still add the facial features and arms and legs.

Ingredients

8 in (20 cm) square cake
1 quantity buttercream (see page 24)
Confectioners' sugar for rolling out fondant on
Water, boiled and cooled for sticking
2 lb (900 g) white fondant
5 oz (150 g) pink fondant
3 1/2 oz (100 g) red fondant
1/3 oz (10 g) black fondant
2 heart shaped cookies (recipe on page 21)
Black food coloring

Equipment

10 in (25 cm) square cake board
Carving knife
Small, sharp, non-serrated knife
Heart template (see page 74)
Carving knife
Palette knife
Rolling pin
Cake smoothers (optional)
Large and small heart-shaped cookie cutters
Small circle cutter or lid
Fine and medium paintbrushes

VALENTINE HEART CUPCAKES

You will need three different sized heart-shaped cutters for this simple yet effective design. Plastic or metal—it doesn't matter although metal cutters will give you a cleaner sharper edge. Roll out a little pink fondant. Keep it fairly thick. Roll out and cut out a smaller, thinner white heart-shape and stick on top. Finish with a small pink heart and pop it on top of a cupcake.

How to Make Your Valentine Heart Cake

Fig. 1

1 Level the cake if necessary and turn it upside down. Place the heart template on top with the point of the heart in one of the corners. Holding your small sharp knife almost vertically, carefully cut around the template (Fig. 1).

2 Slice the cake into two or three layers and fill with buttercream. Reassemble the cake and spread buttercream around the top and sides. Knead and roll out 1 pound 12 ounces (800 g) of white fondant. Carefully lift and place over the cake. Starting with the top of the heart, smooth the icing into place. Trim and neaten around the base.

3 Lightly moisten the exposed cake board with a little water ready to cover it with hearts. To do this you will need about 3 ounces (90 g)each of red, pink, and white fondant. Roll out a little pink fondant and cut out a couple of hearts. Repeat using a little red fondant. Continue until the board is covered allowing the hearts to overlap and rest against the sides of the cake.

4 To make the characters, thinly roll out about 2/3 ounce (20 g) of pink fondant. Cut out a heart-shape using the same cutter that you used to make the cookie itself (Fig. 2). Dab a little water on the back of the pink heart (or the cookie itself) and place the pink heart on top. Smooth it into place. Repeat the procedure to make the second pink cookie heart.

5 To make the lady heart's face, thinly roll out about 1/3 ounce (10 g) of white fondant. Cut out two triangles and stick onto the front of the heart. Make a tiny pink fondant ball shape for her nose and stick in position. Make a tiny red fondant oval for her lips. Pinch the two ends into points and press a tiny line into the top lip and stick it in place.

6 To make the man's face, thinly roll out about 1/3 ounce (10 g) of white fondant and cut out two round discs for his eyes (Fig. 3). Stick them onto the cookie. Add a small pink fondant ball for his nose.

7 Using a little watered down black food coloring and a fine paintbrush, paint the pupils onto the eyes. Add a few extravagant eyelashes to the lady. Paint a smile onto the man's face and a couple of curved lines for his eyebrows.

8 Make two 1/8 ounce (5 g) black fondant oval shapes for the man's feet and stick them onto the board. Roll about 1/2 ounce (15 g) of white fondant into a thin string for his legs. Dab a little water on the cake and lay them in position with the ends resting on the feet.

9 Do the same with the lady heart's legs except this time, leave out the big black boots! Instead tweak the ends into little feet and stick and arrange on the edge of the cake.

10 Place the man heart in position on the legs. To hold him in place, stand a lump of fondant behind him. About 2/3 ounce (20 g) should be sufficient. Use a little water to both stick the fondant to the top of the cake and to the back of the cookie. Repeat with the lady heart.

11 Make four thin pink fondant strings for the arms and stick two onto the side of each heart. I put the man's hand over the top of the lady's so it looks as though they are holding hands.

TIPS: If you're pushed for time just a heart-shaped cookie wrapped in tissue and presented in a pretty box would probably be enough to win somebody's heart. The fact that you baked it yourself should show how much you care.

You can press additional heart shapes into the white fondant covering the cake using the heart cutter if you want just be careful not to go through into the cake itself.

Fig. 2

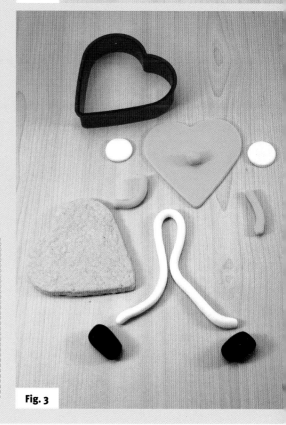

Fig. 3

EASTER BUNNY CAKE

This design would work just as well using chocolates or candies instead of the Easter eggs should you ever have to make a birthday cake for a bunny mad friend or relation!

Ingredients

8 in (20 cm) round cake
2 quantities of chocolate buttercream (see page 24)
Confectioners' sugar for rolling out fondant on
Water, boiled and cooled for sticking fondant together
10 oz (300 g) white fondant
1 oz (30 g) pink fondant
Black food coloring
1 strand raw, uncooked spaghetti (optional)
1 medium-sized chocolate Easter egg (broken)
About 30 mini chocolate eggs

Equipment

10 in (25 cm) round cake board or plate
Small, sharp, non-serrated knife
Fine and medium paintbrushes
Small rolling pin (optional – see step 5)
Carving knife
Palette knife

> **TIPS:** *Add some cookie flowers too to reinforce that Easter feeling*
> *If you don't want to make a whole rabbit, just make his head and the front paws. Press them into the buttercream and he should look as though he's scrambling out of the middle of the cake.*

How to Make Your Easter Bunny Cake

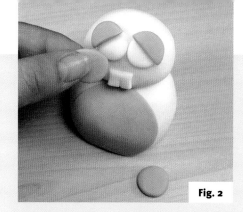

1 Start by making the bunny so he's ready to pop on the cake when it's been frosted. Roll 5 ounces (150 g) of white fondant into an oval for his body (Fig. 1) and stand upright. Dab a little water on the top ready to stick on the head. You could also insert a short length of spaghetti for extra support.

2 Roll 2¹/₂ ounces (75 g) of white fondant into a ball for his head and stick on top of the body. Roll ¹/₂ ounce (15 g) of pink fondant into a ball then squash it into a flat disc and stick onto his tummy.

3 Make two tiny white ball shapes for his eyes. Slightly flatten them and stick them onto the head. For the eyelids, make a tiny pink ball and flatten it. Cut it in half and stick one half over the top of each eye.

4 Make a tiny flat white square for his teeth and make a partial cut across it. Stick it onto the lower part of his face. Make two pink ball shapes for his cheeks. Flatten them and stick them onto the face (Fig. 2). The teeth should be visible. Using the end of your paintbrush poke three dots into each cheek. Make a tiny pink ball for his nose and stick in position.

5 To make the ears roll ¹/₈ ounce (5 g) of white fondant into an oval shape about 2 inches (5 cm) long (Fig. 3). Stick a smaller pink oval on top. Roll over the two together with your small rolling pin to produce a long flat oval about 3 inches (8 cm) long. Use your paintbrush as a mini rolling pin if you don't possess one. Cut the oval in half and stick the ears upright on the head. Allow them to flop over if you wish.

6 Divide about 1¹/₂ ounces (45 g) of white fondant in half and roll into two oval shapes for his feet. Stick them against his body. Make two tiny pink oval shapes and six tiny pink ball shapes. Stick one oval and three tiny ball shapes onto each foot.

7 If you have not already done so, break your Easter egg into pieces. Select two or three attractive bits and place to one side. You may eat the rest!

8 Make two ¹/₃ ounce (10 g) white fondant sausage shapes for his arms and stick against the body with a chunk of Easter egg between them. To finish, paint two black dots with food coloring for his eyes.

9 Prepare the cake by levelling the top and slicing it in half. Spread buttercream over the

Fig. 2

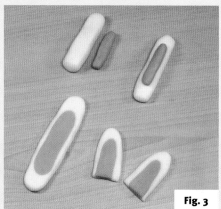

Fig. 3

bottom layer and place the second layer on top. Place the cake on the board or plate, and then coat with a generous covering of chocolate buttercream.

10 Slide a knife underneath the bunny to ensure he's not stuck to your work surface and place towards the rear of the cake. Dab a little chocolate buttercream over his cheeks and paws so it looks as though he's the one who ate the rest of the Easter egg, not you!

11 Arrange the other bits of chocolate egg and a couple of mini eggs on top of the cake and the rest of the mini eggs around the base.

Fig. 1

EASTER BUNNY CUPCAKES

My children informed me that the Easter Bunny can be any color so I made this one pink. Roll about 1 ounce (30 g) of pink fondant into a ball. Roll about ¹/₈ ounce (5 g) of pink fondant into a sausage for his ears and cut in half. Press the end of your paintbrush lengthways into both ears for a bunny shape and stick on top of the head. Add two flattened white fondant ball shapes for eyes and stick two tiny black fondant discs on top. Place a chocolate or candy egg against the body. Make two small fondant sausage shapes for the arms and stick as though holding the egg.

SUMMER HOLIDAY FLOWERS CAKE

A cheerful vase of flowers will brighten up any special occasion—Mother's Day, Easter, a birthday, or simply the start of summer. There are many many ways of making sugar flowers but I thought that these cookies on sticks were bold, striking, and, above all, fairly simple to make.

Ingredients

7 in (18 cm) round sponge cake
1 quantity buttercream (see page 24)
Confectioners' sugar for rolling out
   fondant on
Water, boiled and cooled for sticking
10 flower cookies on sticks (see page 21)
2 lb 4 oz (1 kg) white fondant
1 lb 5 oz (600 g) pink fondant
2 oz (60 g) yellow fondant
Green food color
1 sheet green edible wafer paper

Equipment

10 in (25 cm) round cake board
10 wooden food safe skewers
Carving knife
Palette knife
Rolling pin
Cake smoothers
Small, sharp, non-serrated knife
Cake smoother (optional)
Large and small flower cutters
1 in (2.5 cm) circle cutter (optional)
Paintbrush
Leaf template (page 74)
Pencil
Scissors

> **TIPS:** *Don't panic too much if the fondant gathers into small pleats at the base of the cake. Neaten them as best you can and hide them with the pink fondant when you come to cover the board.*
>
> *Try to resist the urge to snap the skewers to make the flowers different lengths as this can lead to the wood splitting and possible splinters. To vary the flower heights, just alter the amount of skewer you insert into the cake.*

How to Make Your Summer Holiday Flowers Cake

1 Level the top of the cake and slice about 1 inch (2.5 cm) off one side of the cake. This will form the base. Discard (or eat) the smaller piece and stand the cake on its side (Fig. 1).

2 You can slice the cake into layers if you wish but don't cut into more than three or overfill the slices with too much buttercream as this will diminish the strength of the cake. Coat the outside of the cake with buttercream.

3 Knead and roll out 2 pounds (900 g) of white fondant. Carefully cover the cake and starting from the top, smooth the fondant into position. It's an awkward shape and you may find the fondant falling into gathers around the base. If this happens, try to limit the gathers to the back of the cake so the front looks smooth. Trim and neaten around the base.

4 Thinly roll out about 1½ ounces (45 g) of pink fondant. Cut out pink discs and stick around the cake with dabs of water. If you don't possess a circle cutter, make small pink balls and flatten them.

5 Roll 4 ounces (120 g) of pink fondant into a sausage about 13 inches (33 cm) long. Bend it round into a circle and stick on the top of the cake to form the neck of the vase.

6 Lightly moisten the exposed cake board with a little water. Knead and roll out about 12 ounces (350 g) of pink fondant. Lay the fondant around the base of the cake allowing it to fall into folds as you go. Let it rest and fold against the sides of the cake (Fig. 2). The fondant will provide additional support as it dries. You may need to cover the board using three or four sections. Trim and neaten the edges.

7 To decorate a flower, thinly roll out a little pink, yellow, or white fondant and cut out a flower shape using the same size flower cutter that you used to cut out the cookie before baking. Dab a little water on the back of the fondant and place on top of the cookie.

8 Roll out a little pink or yellow fondant and cut out a disc and stick in the center of the flower. Press dots into the flower center using the end of your paintbrush. Using the back of your knife, press three lines into each petal—one long one in the middle and two shorter ones on either side (Fig. 3).

9 Paint about half of the exposed skewer stick with a little green food coloring and allow to dry. Trace and cut out about 12 leaves. When the skewer is dry, thread one or two leaves onto the stem.

10 Repeat making about another nine flowers then carefully poke the stems into your vase.

Fig. 1

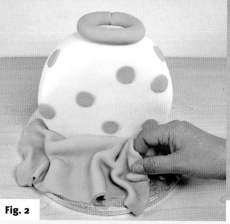
Fig. 2

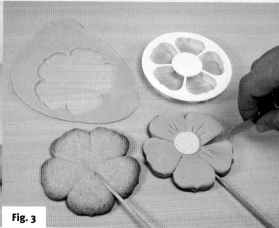
Fig. 3

FLOWER CUPCAKES

Cover and decorate a small flower-shaped cookie as for the main cake and place on top of your cupcake. Cut two leaves out of edible wafer paper and stick one either side of the flower. If you prefer you could make leaves out of green fondant. Thinly roll out a little green fondant and cut out two leaf shapes. Press a line down the center of each leaf with the back of your knife to finish.

SUMMER HOLIDAY BBQ CAKE

This would also make a great cake for Father's Day, an enthusiastic barbecuer's birthday or even 4th of July. I used colored sugar to make the grass around the base of the cake. You could use this on the top too. Just be aware, although it looks bright and vibrant, it does make for a very crunchy topping!

Ingredients
8 in (20 cm) round cake
1 quantity buttercream (see page 24)
Confectioners' sugar for rolling out fondant on
Water, boiled and cooled for sticking
1 lb 14 oz (850 g) white fondant
5 oz (150 g) green fondant
1 lb 8 oz (700 g) golden brown fondant
8 oz (250 g) dark brown fondant

2 oz (60 g) black fondant
1½ oz (45 g) pale blue fondant
1 oz (30 g) flesh-colored fondant
⅓ oz (10 g) gray fondant
1 strand raw, uncooked spaghetti
Yellow and black food coloring
2 oz (60 g) green-colored sugar (see page 28)

Equipment
12 in (30 cm) round cake board
Carving knife
Palette knife
Rolling pin
Cake smoothers (optional)
Small, sharp, non-serrated knife
Paintbrush
8 in (20 cm) round plate or cake board
Number 3 and 2 piping nozzles
2 piping bags (see page 78)
Toothpick (cocktail stick)
Circle cutters 1¾ in and 1½ in (45 mm & 35 mm) optional

> **TIPS:** *You could substitute chocolate-covered finger-shaped cookies for the sausages around the base of the cake if you wanted to cut down on the fondant.*
>
> *Practice making mouths on a spare piece of fondant first before tackling the real thing.*

SUMMER HOLIDAY BBQ CUPCAKES

Hot Dog: Make the hot dog using the instructions from the main cake and place to one side, thinly roll out about 1 ounce (30 g) of white fondant and cut out a 3-inch (8 cm) square. Using watered down red food coloring, paint lines both ways across the square (don't worry about wobbles—it's supposed to be fabric). Dab a little water on the back of the square and place on top of the cupcake. Dab water in the center of the picnic blanket and place your hot dog on top.

Hamburger: To make a hamburger, roll about 1½ ounces (45 g) of brown fondant into a ball. Cut in half. Roll ⅓-ounce (10 g) dark brown fondant into a ball and squash into a disc for the burger. Sandwich this between the two bun halves and press circles into the top of the bun using the end of a drinking straw.

How to Make Your Summer Holiday BBQ Cake

1 Level the top of the cake and turn it upside down. Split and fill the middle of the cake with buttercream. Reassemble the cake and place it on the board. Buttercream the sides and top. Keep the leftover buttercream. Color it yellow and place to one side.

2 Dust your work surface with confectioners' sugar and knead 1 pound 10 ounces (750 g) of white fondant until pliable. Roll it out to a thickness of 1/3 inch (1 cm) and place over the cake.

3 Smooth the top and sides and trim away excess from around the base using a non-serrated knife.

4 Lightly dab a little water over the top of the cake. Thinly roll out the green fondant and place the plate or spare board on top. Holding your knife almost vertically, cut out an eight-inch (20 cm) disc and stick on top of the cake.

5 For a large hot dog, take about 2 1/2 ounces (75 g) of the golden brown fondant and mold it into an oval shape about 3 inches (8 cm) long for the hot dog bun (Fig. 1).

6 Using a knife, make a long cut along the top of the bun and splay the bun open slightly. Roll about 2/3 ounce (20 g) of the darker brown fondant into a sausage about 3 1/2 inches (9 cm) long. Press three short lines into each end of the sausage with the back of your knife.

7 Dab a little water inside the bun and lay the sausage inside. Dab a little water on the cake board and place the hot dog on the board beside the cake. I found it best to do this straight away so the bun could fit itself around the curve of the cake.

8 Make about eight more hot dogs and arrange around the cake. While you have the colors out, make eight small hot dogs for the man to hold.

9 Next, move to the man and begin with his feet. Roll two 1/8 ounce (5 g) lumps of black fondant into oval shapes (Fig. 2) and stick them on top of the hot dogs around the base.

10 Roll 1 1/2 ounces (45 g) of blue fondant into a sausage about 7 inches (18 cm) long for his legs. Cut off the rounded ends and bend the sausage into a "U" shape. With the ankles resting on the shoes, stick the legs onto the cake.

11 Make a 1 1/2 ounce (45 g) white fondant oval shape for his body. Stick on top of his legs. Insert a section of spaghetti if you wish to give added support. Leave about 1 inch (2.5 cm) protruding on which to slot his head.

12 Make a 1/2 ounce (15 g) flesh-colored triangle shape for his head and stick on top of his body. Flatten the top of the head slightly to make it ready for the chef's hat.

13 Make two tiny white discs for his eyes and stick on to the face. Make a flesh-colored disc for his eyelids. Cut it in half and stick one half at an angle over each eye. Add a tiny flesh-colored ball shape for his nose.

14 To make the mouth, press the edge of a circle cutter or piping nozzle (tip) into the lower part of the man's head. Press it in then pull downwards slightly before pulling the cutter out completely. Your man should now be sporting a goofy smile. Stick a tiny white fondant rectangle inside the mouth for his teeth.

15 To make the hair, dip a tiny bit of dark brown fondant in water and work it in your fingers until it's a bit of a gooey mess. Carefully smear it around the top of his head. Use the tip of your paintbrush and a toothpick to "style" it (Fig. 3).

16 Make the chef's hat by rolling about 1/8 ounce (5 g) of white fondant into an oval. Slice off the two rounded ends and stick on top of the head. Any protruding spaghetti should now be hidden. If it's not, snap it off. Make a small white ball, flatten it and stick on top of the hat.

17 Make two tiny flesh-colored ball shapes for the ears. Stick one either side of his head and poke a small hollow into each one with the end of your paintbrush. Paint two black food color dots on the eyes.

18 For the arms, roll 2/3 ounce (20 g) of white fondant into a sausage about 4 1/2 inches (11.5 cm) long and cut in half.

19 Take two of the tiny hot dogs you made earlier and gently press and stick them onto his chest. Bend one arm into a right angle and with the rounded end forming the shoulder, stick against the left hand side of the figure. Take a small ball of flesh-colored fondant and flatten slightly. Stick on the end of the arm.

20 Press another hotdog on the body and stick the second arm and hand in position. All the hot dogs should be held in place securely.

21 To make the barbecue, roll 1 1/2 ounces (45 g) of black fondant into a ball and either squash it or use a circle cutter to produce a thick disc about 2 inches (5 cm) in diameter.

22 Using the smaller circle cutter press a circular imprint just inside the top of the barbecue. If you don't have a cutter, use the tip of your knife. Press seven or eight lines across the top of the barbecue using the back of your knife.

23 Stick the barbecue in position on the cake and make and stick three tiny dark brown sausages on top. Make the tongs by rolling a little bit of gray fondant into a thin string about 2 inches (5 cm) long. Flatten both ends and fold the tongs into a "V" shape and stick next to the barbecue.

24 Put some yellow frosting into a piping bag fitted with a number 3 piping tip. Alternatively close the bag and snip a tiny triangle off the corner. Pipe "mustard" onto the large hotdogs. Repeat with another piping bag and a smaller (no. 2) tip on the smaller hotdogs. If you don't want to pipe, roll strings of yellow fondant instead.

25 Roll the leftover gray fondant into a ball and flatten it to make a plate. Stick this onto the cake and pile the rest of the tiny hot dogs on top.

26 Carefully spoon the colored sugar around the cake board. Use a soft paintbrush to ease it between the hotdogs.

Fig. 1

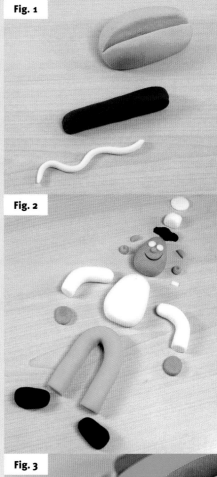

Fig. 2

Fig. 3

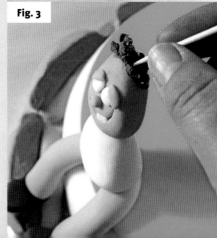

53

THANKSGIVING TURKEY CAKE

I've made the odd exotic cake in my time but the excitement that a large chocolate crispy cake produced in my house you'd have to see to believe. They couldn't wait for it to be photographed so they could eat it! I piped royal icing around the top and base of the actual main cake to give it a slightly formal air. I thought it would contrast nicely with the overweight cartoon turkey who appears to have crushed the cake. If you don't want to pipe, you could leave it plain or stick small candies or a bit of ribbon around the base instead.

Ingredients
7 in (18 cm) round sponge cake
1 quantity buttercream (see page 24)
3 oz (90 g) cereal
7 oz (200 g) milk chocolate
1 lb 14 oz (850 g) white fondant
1 lb 10 oz (750 g) dark brown fondant
1 oz (30 g) golden brown fondant
1/8 oz (5 g) black fondant
Confectioners' sugar for rolling out fondant on
Water, boiled and cooled for sticking fondant
2-3 tablespoons of white royal icing or white frosting (optional—see introduction above)
3 sheets edible wafer paper (I found some orange-colored wafer paper but plain white will work just as well)
1 teaspoon cocoa powder

Equipment
10 in (25 cm) round cake board
Heatproof mixing bowl
Spoon
Baking, greaseproof, or wax paper
Scissors
1 1/2 pint (3/4 liter) pudding bowl. (Use a larger bowl and increase the ingredients if you are making a bigger cake—your bird needs to look ridiculously big when placed on the cake)
Carving knife
Palette knife
Rolling pin
Cake smoother
Small, sharp, non-serrated knife
Piping bag fitted with star nozzle (tip)
Paintbrush
Round lid or circle cutter about 1 in (2.5 cm) diameter
Saucer or plate about the size of the diameter of the bowl the turkey's body was created in.
Tail feather template (see page 74)
Pencil

TIPS: *Hasten the hardening time of the turkey's body by placing the bowl of chocolate cereal in the freezer for about twenty minutes.*
If your beak starts to slip, partially insert a toothpick into the cereal below the beak to hold it in place while it's drying. Remove it before serving the cake.

How to Make Your Thanksgiving Turkey Cake

Fig. 1

1 Melt the chocolate in a mixing bowl (see page 21) and stir in the cereal. Cut out a small baking parchment disc and place in the bottom of the bowl that you're using to form the turkey's body (Fig. 1). Spoon the chocolate cereal mixture into the bowl and allow it to set.

2 Level the sponge cake and split it in half. Fill with buttercream and reassemble. Place in the center of the board and coat the outside with buttercream. Cover the cake using about 1 pound 8 ounces (700 g) of white fondant. Smooth the top and sides and trim and neaten the base. Keep any excess buttercream.

3 Moisten the exposed cake board and cover the board using about 5 ounces (150 g) of white fondant. Use the bandage method shown on page 28.

4 Place about two tablespoons of royal icing or white frosting into the piping bag and pipe a line of shells around the top and base of the cake. Squeeze a little out, release the pressure and pull back slightly so the shell tapers into a thin tail. Squeeze again, release and repeat round the cake. Practice on your worktop first if you're unsure. Place the cake to one side.

5 If the turkey's body has set, gently poke a palette knife down the side of the bowl to loosen the chocolate mixture. Turn it out and remove the greaseproof disc.

6 Roll about 4 ounces (120 g) of the dark brown fondant into a ball for his head (Fig. 2). Flatten it slightly and press onto the body. A light dab of water or buttercream should hold it in place.

7 Make two 1/3 ounces (10 g) dark brown fondant carrot shapes for the wings. Flatten slightly and make two partial cuts into the widest part of each wing. Stick one on either side of the body.

8 Make two white fondant ball shapes for eyes. Flatten them and stick onto the face. Add two smaller black fondant balls and two tiny white fondant dots for highlights.

9 Roll about 2/3 ounce (20 g) of the golden brown fondant into a sort of carrot shape for his beak. Using a lid, circle cutter, or the tip of your knife, press a curved line into the beak. Carefully stick it onto the face. You will be fighting gravity so don't use too much water to stick it or it will slide off.

10 Take the saucer and decide where on the cake you would like your turkey to sit. Press the saucer down hard so the cake starts to crumble (Fig. 3). When you have demolished enough, remove the saucer.

11 Roll the remaining golden brown fondant into two little carrot shapes for the feet. Make two cuts into the widest part of each foot and press a couple of lines across each claw with the back of your knife.

12 Stick the claws on the edge of the cake and place the turkey's body on top.

13 Trace and cut out 5 edible wafer tail feath-

Fig. 2

Fig. 3

ers. Dip your finger in a little cocoa powder and rub a little onto the end of each feather. Stick the feathers on the rear of the turkey with a little buttercream.

THANKSGIVING TURKEY CUPCAKES

Fill the cupcake case with chocolate crispy mixture. Roll about 1 ounce (30 g) of brown colored fondant into a ball for his head and stick in place. Make a small lighter brown carrot shape for his beak and bend the end into a curve. Stick onto the head. Make two tiny white fondant balls for his eyes and stick onto the head. Paint two black food color dots onto the eyes. Cut out four or five edible wafer paper tail feathers (template on page 74) and insert into the back of the cupcake case.

A HALLOWEEN COSTUMES CAKE

I used a gold-colored cake board for this design because the color nicely complements the orange/black theme of the cake. If you can't get one, silver would work just as well. You could also use a decorated Halloween plate that often appear during October.

How to Make Your Halloween Costumes Cake

1 Level the top of your cake if necessary and turn it upside down. Split the cake in half and fill the middle with buttercream. Reassemble the cake and place it in the middle of the cake board. Coat the top and sides with buttercream.
2 Dust your work surface with icing sugar to prevent the fondant from sticking. Knead 1 pound 10 ounces (750 g) of fondant until soft and pliable. Roll it out to a thickness of about 1/4 inch (5 mm). Lift the fondant and place over the cake. Smooth the top and sides into position and cut away any excess from the base.
3 Wrap and keep about 1/8 ounce (5 g) of the orange fondant for his socks later. Roll the rest into a ball shape for the pumpkin. Press vertical lines around the side of the pumpkin with the back of your knife (Fig. 1). Stick the pumpkin on the top of the cake with a light dab of water. Slice a little off the top of the pumpkin for the hat and place to one side so you can use it later.
4 Roll 1 ounce (30 g) of flesh-colored fondant into a ball for the child's head (Fig. 2). Slice a little off the top and bottom and stick the head on top of the pumpkin. Roll the cut off bits into two thin strings about 1 inch (2.5 cm) long for his legs. Stick the legs at the base of the pumpkin.
5 Make three tiny flesh-colored ball shapes. Stick one on his face for his nose and the other two on the side of his head for ears. Poke the end of a paintbrush into each ear to make a small hollow. Make two tiny white fondant ball shapes for eyes and stick on the face.
6 To make the cut out face on the pumpkin itself, thinly roll out about 1/3 ounce (10 g) of black fondant. Cut out three triangles for the eyes and nose and stick them in position. Cut out 6 smaller triangles and stick in a curve to make the pumpkin's smile.
7 Place a dab of water on the child's head and stick the pumpkin hat in place. Make a tiny green fondant sausage shape for the stalk. Slice both rounded ends off the green sausage and stick it upright on top of the hat.
8 Divide the left over orange fondant in two for his socks. Roll each half into an oval shape and stick one at the bottom of each leg. Press a few lines across both socks using the back of your knife.
9 Roll 1/8 ounce (5 g) of black fondant into two oval shapes for his shoes. Stick one at the end of each foot and press a line across the sole of each shoe to give the impression of a heel.
10 To make the ghost, roll 1 1/2 ounce (45 g) of white fondant into an oval shape for the body (Fig. 3). Stick it upright on the cake near the pumpkin. You could insert a little spaghetti down the center of the oval if you wish to provide extra support.
11 Roll about 1/8 ounce (5 g) of black fondant into a thin sausage about 3 1/2 inches (9 cm) long for his legs. Cut it in half and stick in front of the body. Roll 1/8 ounce (5 g) black fondant into two oval shapes for his shoes and stick onto the end of his feet as before.
12 Roll 2 ounces (60 g) of white fondant into a ball then flatten and roll it out to make a disc about 5 inches (13 cm) in diameter. Lightly moisten the body and place the disc over the top allowing it to fall into soft pleats or folds.
13 Stick two tiny white ball shapes on the front of the ghost and paint two black food color dots on the eyes. Do the same on pumpkin boy.
14 Dab a little watered down green food color around the top of the cake to look like grass.
15 Place ribbon round the base of the cake and secure at the back with a little sticky tape. Glue some around the edge of the baseboard, if you wish.

TIP: *When making the pumpkin's mouth, I found it best to paint a light curved line of water on the front of the pumpkin. This gave me a guide to follow when sticking the teeth in place.*

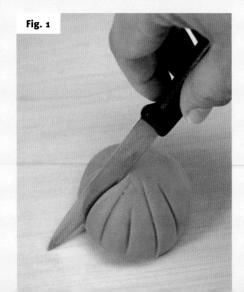

Fig. 1

Fig. 2

Fig. 3

Ingredients

8 in (20 cm) round cake
1 quantity of buttercream (see page 24)
Confectioners' sugar for rolling out fondant on
Water, boiled and cooled for sticking fondant
2 lb (900 g) white fondant
7 oz (200 g) orange-colored fondant
1½ oz (45 g) flesh-colored fondant
1 oz (30 g) black fondant
⅛ oz (5 g) green fondant
1 strand raw uncooked spaghetti
Black & green food color gels or pastes

Equipment

10 in (25 cm) round cake board
Carving knife
Palette knife
Rolling pin
Cake smoothers (optional)
Small, sharp, non-serrated knife
Fine and medium paintbrushes
Tape measure
Ribbon – 28 inches (71 cm) for the cake,
   33 inches (84 cm) for the cake board
Scissors
Sticky tape
Non-toxic glue stick (optional)

TIP: *If you think your children will be able
to resist eating the figures, make them on
a thin cake card like the one used in Baby's
First Birthday on page 30. They can then
be easily removed and kept.*

HALLOWEEN CUPCAKES

Pumpkin: Roll about 1½ ounces (45 g) of orange-colored fondant into a ball. Press vertical lines around the sides of the ball using the back of your knife. Make a tiny green sausage shape for the stalk and stick on top. Place about a tablespoon of green-colored buttercream on top of the cupcake and rough it up with a fork to look like grass. Place the pumpkin on top.

Ghost: To make a little ghost, roll about ⅔ ounce (20 g) of white fondant into an oval. Stand it upright and dab a little water on the top. Thinly roll out about 1 ounce (30 g) of white fondant and cut out a 3-inch (8 cm) disc Place on top of the oval allowing it to fall into folds. Paint two black food color eyes on the front of the ghost.

A HALLOWEEN SPIDER CAKE

Although not perhaps a design a hardened arachnophobe might like, I think the spiders on this cake are actually quite amusing. I also think that limiting the colors to orange, black, and white makes this a very striking cake. If you wanted to make your spiders scarier, you could pipe some white fangs onto the sides of their mouths and paint red food color veins on their eyes. You could also color the sponge cake inside a blood curdling red or disgusting green color before baking.

Ingredients

8 in (20 cm) round sponge
1 quantity of buttercream (see page 24)
Confectioners' sugar for rolling out
   fondant on
Water, boiled and cooled for sticking fondant
2 lb 4 oz (1 kg) orange colored fondant
1 lb 2 oz (500 g) black fondant
2¹/₂ oz (75 g) white fondant
Licorice (laces, pipes, tubes, or even
   un-wound wheels will work)

Equipment

12 in (30 cm) round cake board
Pastry brush
Rolling pin
Small, sharp, non-serrated knife
Cake smoothers (optional)
Plastic wrap
Carving knife
Palette knife
Spatula or pancake turner or fish slice
Clean ruler or long knife
65 in (165 cm) black ribbon
Scissors
Sticky tape
Metal piping nozzle (tip)— any design
Medium paintbrush

HALLOWEEN SPIDER CUPCAKES

Make a spider (as large or small as you want) using the same instructions as for the main cake. Pipe or spread orange-colored buttercream onto the top of your cupcake and place the spider on top.

How to Make Your Halloween Spider Cake

Fig. 1

Fig. 2

Fig. 3

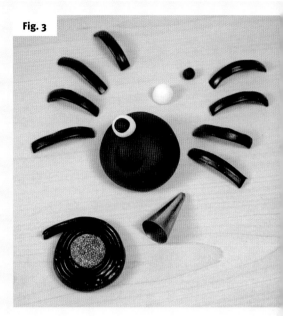

1 Using the pastry brush, lightly dab water over the entire cake board. Knead and roll out 10 ounces (300 g) of the orange fondant. Lift and place the fondant onto the dampened board and continue rolling up to and over the edges of the board. Neaten the edges and place the board to one side. Place a sheet of plastic wrap over the top to stop the fondant from drying out too much.

2 Level the cake and turn it upside down. Slice and fill the center with buttercream. Reassemble the cake and coat the outside of the cake with buttercream.

3 Knead and roll out 1 pound 8 ounces (700 g) of the orange fondant to about a thickness of 1/3 inch (1 cm). Don't go any thinner as you'll be pressing into the fondant later and you won't want the cake covering to split. Lift and place over the cake. Smooth the top and sides and trim and neaten around the base.

4 Remove the plastic wrap from the board and using a large spatula, carefully lift and place the cake off center on the covered board (Fig. 1).

5 To make the main support spokes of the web, press four lines across the top of the cake using a ruler or back of a knife (Fig. 2). You should end up with something that looks like a star. Press deeply enough to leave an impression but not so hard that you go right through to the cake.

6 Holding the ruler or knife vertically, continue the lines down the side of the cake. Your cake

should now look as though it has been divided up into eight very large portions. Then press and continue the lines in the fondant on the cake board.

7 Now you need to fill in the web. Using the back of your small knife, press a line into the fondant between two of the spokes. Press another between the next two spokes. Continue until you have created an octagon. Repeat until your web fills the top of the cake.

8 Neaten the join between cake and board by placing black ribbon around the base. Use a little sticky tape to secure the join at the back.

9 To make a large spider, roll 3 ounces (90 g) of black fondant into a ball (Fig. 9). Holding a piping nozzle at an angle, press a smile into the body.

10 Cut 8 bits of licorice about 1 1/2 inches (4 cm) long for legs. Poke them in the body. Stick the spider onto the cake with a dab of water.

11 Make two 1/8 ounce (5 g) white fondant ball shapes for his eyes and stick above the mouth. Stick two tiny flattened black fondant ball shapes on to the white.

12 Make another three big spiders and stick onto the cake and board. I then made one using 1 1/2 ounces (45 g) of black fondant for the body, two using 2/3 ounce (20 g) and 3 tiny ones using 1/8 ounce (5g) but obviously you can make your spiders any size you want.

13 To finish, stick the remaining black ribbon around the edge of the board.

TIPS: *Wet black fondant can get messy. Resist the urge to brush away sugar marks until the cake is finished. Then brush away any sugar dust using a soft damp paintbrush. Leave the cake to dry.*

At this time of year all sorts of ghoulish candies appear in the shops. You could stick a few edible eyeballs, teeth or even a sugar bat in your web.

A SLEDDING SANTA CAKE

I found it easiest to make the Santa beforehand so he was ready to pop on the cake when the slope was prepared. Make him up on a separate board dusted with a little confectioners' sugar so he doesn't stick. Slide a knife under him when you need to move him to release him and let him face the terrifying edible slope of your delicious cake! The ingredients vary slightly depending on whether you are using a fruit or sponge cake as a base.

Ingredients
7 in (18 cm) square sponge cake
2 quantities soft white frosting (not royal
     icing) (see page 25)
or
7 in (18 cm) square fruit cake
3-4 tablespoons apricot jam
1 lb 8 oz (700 g) marzipan (almond paste)
2 quantities royal icing (do not use
     buttercream or the soft white frosting) (see
     page 24)

For both cakes:
Confectioners' sugar for rolling out fondant on
Water, boiled and cooled for sticking fondant
2 oz (60 g) brown fondant
2^1/$_2$ oz (75 g) red fondant
3 oz (90 g) black fondant
1 oz (30 g) flesh-colored fondant
1 oz (30 g) white fondant
^{1}/$_3$ oz (10 g) orange-colored fondant
6 oz (175 g) green fondant
1 strand raw uncooked spaghetti

Equipment
12 in (30 cm) square board
Rolling pin
Plastic wrap
Small, sharp, non-serrated knife
Fine and medium paintbrushes
Carving knife
Palette knife
Ruler
Toothpick (cocktail stick) for making fir trees
Scissors
Sieve

SANTA CUPCAKES

Because red buttercream has a tendency to get everywhere I found it easier to make the head off the cupcake and to put it in place once he was finished. Use the same instructions for head as given in the main cake but make his beard slightly shorter. It means it's less likely to break when you're lifting it on to the top of the cupcake.

How to Make Your Sledding Santa Cake

Fig. 1

Fig. 3

1 Roll the brown fondant into an oval and squash to a thickness of about 1/3 inch (1 cm). Tweak the front into an upwards point. Use a bit of scrunched up plastic wrap to support it while it's drying (Fig. 1).

2 To make Santa, roll 1 ounce (30 g) of red fondant into a sausage about 5 inches (13 cm) long. Slice the rounded ends off and bend the rest into a "U" shape for his legs (Fig. 2). Stick towards the rear of the sled.

3 Make two 1/3 ounce (10 g) black fondant "L" shapes for his boots and stick one on the end of each leg.

4 Make a 1 ounce (30 g) red fondant oval for his body and stick on top of the legs. Insert a bit of spaghetti for support if you wish.

5 Make the trim around his coat by rolling 2/3 ounce (20 g) of white fondant into a sausage about 7 inches (18 cm) long. Lay and stick this around the base of the body. Poke a few hollows into the trim with the end of your paintbrush.

6 Make a 2/3 ounce (20 g) flesh-colored fondant ball for his head and stick on top of the body.

7 Thinly roll out about 1/8 ounce (5 g) of white fondant and press lines into it using the back of your knife. Cut out a triangle for his beard and stick on the front of the face. Poke a hollow for his mouth with the end of your paintbrush.

8 Make two tiny white fondant diamond shapes for his mustache. Flatten them slightly and press lines into them with the back of your knife. Stick them above the mouth.

9 Make three tiny flesh-colored ball shapes for his ears and nose. Stick all three in position and poke a hollow in the ears with the end of your paintbrush.

10 Make two tiny white fondant ball shapes for his eyes. Squash them flat and stick onto the face. Stick a tiny speck of white fondant at an angle either side of each eye for his eyebrows.

11 Make a 1/8 ounce (5 g) red fondant triangle for his hat and stick on top of his head. Use about 1/8 ounce (5 g) of white fondant to make a sausage for the trim and a ball for the pom pom. Poke a few hollows in both with the end of your paintbrush.

12 Roll about 1/3 ounce (10 g) of red fondant into a sausage about 3 inches (8 cm) long for his arms. Cut it in two and stick one either side of his body. You could position the arms how you want but I thought they looked amusing sloping backwards as though he was holding on to the back of the sled.

13 Add two tiny flesh-colored ball shapes for his hands and stick on to the ends of the arms. Paint a tiny dot on to his eyes with black food coloring. Place Santa to one side.

14 To shape the cake, if you are using a sponge cake, lay it flat and make a mark half-way along one side. Cut the cake from the opposite corner to the mark and remove the cutaway triangle (Fig 3).

15 Stand the big section of cake on its side. Turn the cutaway triangle around and butt it up against the main cake. You should now have a long triangular cake.

16 Stand the cake diagonally across the cake board. Coat it with soft with icing. Use your palette knife to spread it over the cake and board. Place Santa onto the slope.

17 If you are using fruitcake, cut and shape the cake into a triangle following instructions for sponge cake. Place it diagonally on the board. Paint the cake with the apricot jam and roll out and cover the cake with the marzipan. Patch any tears or gaps with additional marzipan. Smooth it as best you can. It does not have to be perfect. Then cover with the royal icing.

18 To finish, make a couple of penguins (instructions given in Skiing Snowman Cake on page 72) and 11 or 12 fir trees (instructions given in Christmas Skating Cake on page 67). Place a little confectioners' sugar in a sieve and tap gently over the tops of the fir trees.

> **TIPS:** *If a sloping cake looks too complicated, use a normal round or square cake instead and place him on the top.*
>
> *Make sure when you're making your slope that it is wide enough for the sled to sit on.*

Fig. 2

A CHRISTMAS SKATING CAKE

This would make a really unusual Christmas cake. Lose the red hats and it would work for other times of the year too. I was tempted to put skating boots on the penguin too. Talking of penguins, the instructions for making him are given in Skiing Snowman on page 68.

Ingredients
7 in (18 cm) round sponge cake
1 quantity buttercream (see page 24)
or
7 in (18 cm) round fruitcake
3-4 tablespoons apricot jam
1 lb 5 oz (600 g) marzipan (almond paste)

For both types of cake you will also need:
Confectioners' sugar for rolling out fondant on
Cooled, boiled water for sticking fondant
2 lb 7¹/₂ oz (1.1 kg) white fondant
2¹/₂ oz (75 g) flesh-colored fondant
4¹/₂ oz (135 g) green fondant
2 oz (60 g) red fondant
1 oz (30 g) black fondant
¹/₈ oz (5 g) orange-colored fondant
Blue and black food coloring
1 sheet of white edible wafer paper
Black food color pen
1 strand raw, dried spaghetti

Equipment
12 in (30 cm) round cake board
Toothpick (cocktail stick)
Fine and medium paint brushes

Rolling pin
Cake smoothers (optional)
Small, sharp, non-serrated knife
Carving knife
Palette knife
Metal spatula (fish slice)
Scissors
Piping nozzle (tip) any design
Cheeky drinking straw
    (see page 11)
Sieve

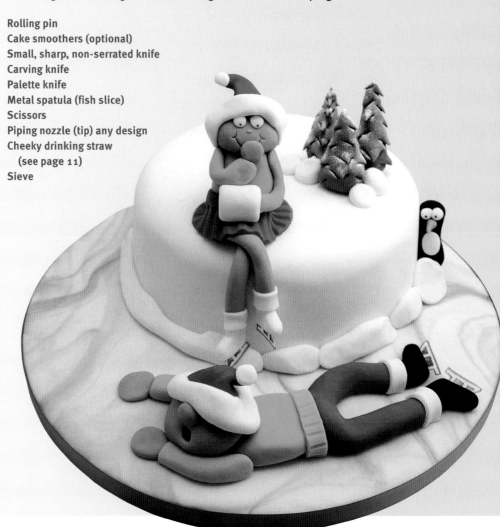

CHRISTMAS SKATING CUPCAKE

Cover the cupcakes with discs of marbled blue fondant. Trace and cut out two edible wafer paper ice skating blades (page 74) and place to one side. Make two ¹/₈ ounce (5 g) blue fondant "L" shapes for the boots. Press lines across the front of the boots to look like laces. Position and stick the boots on top of the cupcake. Press a blade into the base of each boot. Using either a piping bag with a number 1 piping nozzle (tip) and a little buttercream or royal icing, or a tube of writing icing, pipe two wiggly laces onto each boot.

How to Make Your Christmas Skating Cake

1 Lightly moisten the whole of the cake board with water and place to one side. Take a 12 ounce (350 g) lump of white fondant and apply a few streaks of blue food color to it using a toothpick. Partially knead the color into the fondant until you see a marbled effect start to occur then start to roll the fondant out on your work surface.

2 Lift and place the marbled fondant onto the cake board. Continue rolling up to and over the edges of the board. Smooth the surface and trim the excess away from the edges. Place the board to one side.

3 If using a sponge cake, level the cake and turn it upside down. Split and fill the middle with buttercream. Reassemble the cake and spread buttercream around the top and sides. Cover using 1 pound 5 ounces (600 g) white fondant then place off center on the board. If using a fruitcake, level the top and place upside down on the board. Heat the apricot jam in a microwave in a heatproof bowl for a couple of minutes then spread over the top and sides. Cover with the marzipan. Moisten the covered cake with a little water then cover using 1 pound 5 ounces (600 g) of white fondant. Lift and place off center on the board

4 Break about 2¹/₂ ounces (75 g) of white fondant into irregular oval shapes and stick around the base of the cake.

5 Make the sitting skater's legs by rolling ¹/₂ ounce (15 g) of flesh-colored fondant into a string about 6¹/₂ inches (16.5 cm) long (Fig. 1). Stick this onto the edge of the cake, crossing the legs at the knees.

6 Using the black food color pen and edible wafer paper, trace and cut out four skate blades (page 74). Place to one side. Cut a ¹/₈ ounce (5 g) ball of white fondant in half to make the boots. Roll each half into an "L" shape and press a blade into each base. Stick one onto the end of each leg. Thinly roll out a little white fondant and cut out two tiny rectangles about ¹/₄ x 1 inch (1 x 2.5 cm). Stick one over the top of each boot to hide the join between boot and leg.

7 Roll 1 ounce (30 g) of green fondant into an oval for her body and stick upright on top of the legs. Insert a strand of spaghetti for support. Thinly roll out ¹/₂ ounce (15 g) of red fondant and cut out a rectangle about 4¹/₂ x ³/₄ inch (11.5 x 2 cm) for her skirt. Press lines into the skirt with the end of your paintbrush. Lay and stick the skirt around her body and legs.

8 Make a ¹/₃ ounce (10 g) flesh ball for her head and stick on top of the body. Press a piping nozzle into the fondant to make a smile and using a cheeky drinking straw add a little curve at both ends of the mouth. Add two flattened white fondant balls for eyes and a tiny bit of flesh-colored fondant for a nose.

9 Make a ¹/₈ ounce (5 g) red fondant triangle for her hat and stick on top of her head. Roll ¹/₃ ounce (10 g) of white fondant into a long sausage and lay and stick around the base of the hat. Stick a tiny white ball on the tip of the hat.

10 Roll about ¹/₈ ounce (5 g) of white fondant into an oval for her hand muff. Slice the two rounded ends off and stick it on her lap. Roll ¹/₈ ounce (5 g) of green fondant into a sausage about 3¹/₂ inches (9 cm) long for her arms. Cut it in half and bending both arms at the elbows, stick them in position. Make a tiny flesh-colored ball shape for her hand and flatten it. Position it so that it's on the end of the arm and over the mouth.

11 To make the fallen skater, roll 1 ounce (30 g) of red fondant into a sausage about 6¹/₂ inches (16.5 cm) long for his legs (Fig. 2). Bend it into a "U" shape and stick it on to the board. Make two ¹/₈ ounce (5 g) black "L" shaped boots and stick one on the end of each leg. Insert a blade into the base of each boot and add a white cuff as before.

12 Roll 1 ounce (30 g) of green fondant into an oval for his body. Butt it up to the top of the red trousers and stick it onto the board. Thinly roll out a little green fondant and cut out a thin strip. Press lines into it using the back of your knife and lay and stick over the base of the jumper to hide the join.

13 Roll ¹/₂ ounce (15 g) of green fondant into a sausage about 4³/₄ inches (12 cm) long for his arms. Cut it in half and stick the arms on the board. Make two flesh-colored fondant ball shapes for hands. Squash them and stick one on the end of each arm.

14 Make a 1 ounce (30 g) flesh-colored ball for his head and stick on to body. It should also rest on the arms. Make a mouth by pressing the end of a paintbrush into his face and pulling downwards. Add a flesh-colored ball for his nose and a hat as before.

15 To make the trees, knead 1¹/₂ ounces (45 g) of green fondant and ¹/₈ ounce (5 g) of black fondant together and divide into three. Roll each third into a carrot shape. Poke a toothpick into the base so you can hold it and and snip around the sides with scissors to make the branches (Fig. 3). Remove the toothpick and place the tree on top of the cake. Add a few white fondant snowballs and a penguin or two as well if you like.

16 Sift a little confectioners' sugar snow over the top of the fir trees.

> **TIPS:** *Allow the two ends of the girl's skirt to cross over and lie on the cake behind her back. If you force the skirt round her waist it might tear. The important thing is that it looks good from the front.*
>
> *Use a large flat metal pancake turner to help you lift the cake on to the covered board. You are less likely to get fingerprints in the side of the cake.*

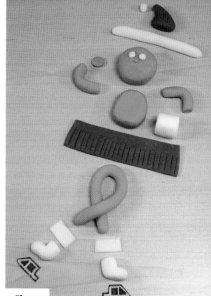

Fig. 1

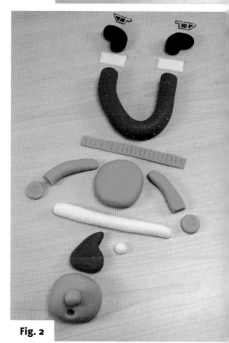

Fig. 2

Fig. 3

NAUGHTY REINDEER CAKE

After years of pulling a sleigh with a great big sack in the back, Santa's reindeers were getting a bit curious and wanted to know what was actually in there. If you're using fruitcake then read the TIPS before you start. To give this cake height I used two cakes: 7 and 6 inches (18 and 15 cm) round. If you don't possess these exact size baking pans then use what pans you have and either trim the cakes to size or simply make a slightly larger or smaller version.

Ingredients
7 and 6 in (18 and 15 cm) round cakes.
2 quantities of buttercream (see page 24)
Confectioners' sugar for rolling out
   fondant on
Water, boiled and cooled for sticking fondant
2 lbs 4 oz (1 kg) brown fondant
4 oz (120 g) red fondant
5 oz (150 g) white fondant
Dark brown & black food color pastes

Equipment
10 in (25 cm) round cake board
Carving knife
Palette knife
Rolling pin
Small, sharp, non-serrated knife
Fine and medium paintbrushes
Tape measure
Plastic wrap
Toothpick (cocktail stick)

NAUGHTY REINDEER CUPCAKE

Make your batch (or should that be herd?) of reindeer cake toppers before frosting the cupcakes. Make a small brown fondant oval for the reindeer's body and a head and two legs using the instructions given for the main cake. Pipe or spread snowy white frosting over the top of your cupcake and partially submerge your reindeer in it.

How to Make Your Naughty Reindeer Cake

1 Level the top of the largest cake. Slice both cakes in half and split and fill with buttercream. Reassemble both cakes and spread buttercream over their tops and sides. Place the largest cake in the center of the board and place the smaller one on top (Fig. 1).

2 Carve a little off the top edge of the larger cake to soften the sharp edge and spread a layer of buttercream over any exposed bits of sponge. Carve a few lumps and bumps out of the cakes too if you like.

3 Measure the height of the cake and make a note of the measurement. Knead the light brown fondant until pliable then roll it out and cut out a long thick strip about 23 x 7 inches (58 x 18 cm). The width of the strip must be higher than the height of the cake.

4 Carefully wind the icing up and, holding it vertically, unwind it around the cake (Fig. 2). Smooth it into position and tweak the top into folds. Neaten the join and base and cover the leftover light brown fondant.

5 Make a line of stitching down the center of the bag by pressing a line of shallow cuts with the tip of your knife. Using the end of your paintbrush poke a line of hollows around the top of the bag ready for the bag's cord.

6 Wrap and put about 1/2 ounce (15g) of the light brown icing to one side so you can use it for the antlers and noses later. Color the rest of the brown fondant a darker shade of brown for the reindeer themselves. (You will need about 12 ounces / 350 g)

7 Make four 1 1/2 ounces (45 g) dark brown fondant oval shapes for the bodies (Fig. 3) and stick them into the top of the bag. You can arrange them in whatever positions you like. I put three standing upright and one pointing downwards into the bag itself.

8 Using about 2/3 ounce (20 g) of brown fondant for each head, make three heads. Roll the fondant into a sausage shape and squeeze the center slightly. Pinch two ears into one end and stick a head onto each of the upright bodies. (This is also how you would make a hippopotamus'

head should you ever be asked to make one!)

9 Poke a hollow into the lower part of Rudolph's face with the end of your paintbrush to make a mouth. Make another head or half head and place inside the bag, Fill any other gaps in the top of the bag with heads, legs, or even presents or snowballs if you want.

10 To make the back leg for the reindeer clambering into the bag, take 1/8 ounce (5 g) of brown fondant and mold it into a shape that looks a bit like a tennis racquet. With the leg lying flat, bend the rounded end towards the straight section. Stick the leg onto the side of the deer and make a second one for the other side.

11 Make thin string shapes for the front legs of the other reindeers and stick them in different positions. Make a tiny diamond shape for a tail and press a few lines into it with your knife. Stick on the rear of the climbing deer.

12 Make eight tiny white fondant ball shapes for the deer's eyes and stick two on each head. Using the lighter brown fondant, make round ball shaped noses for all of the deer whose faces are visible (except for Rudolph).

13 To make a set of antlers, roll a tiny sausage of light brown fondant and dab a little water on a reindeer's head. Place the sausage on the top of the head and press gently down with the nonbrush end of your paintbrush. The antler should automatically bend into a "U" shape though you may need to tweak it slightly with the softer brush end.

14 Using a fine paintbrush or a toothpick, paint a black food coloring dot on each eye. Make a tiny red ball shape for Rudolph's nose and stick it on his face.

15 To make the bag's cord, take a small bit of the red fondant and roll it into a thin string about 2 inches (5 cm) long. Press lines across it using the back of your knife and stick so it hangs in a "U" shape between two of the holes in the top of the bag. Repeat around the top of the bag.

16 Make two longer strings for the front of the bag and stick in place. To make the tassels, roll out a little red fondant and cut out two long

Fig. 3

triangles. Cut a few lines into each one and stick on to the ends of the cords. Allow the strands to splay slightly. To finish stick a tiny red fondant ball on top and press a few lines into it with the back of your knife.

17 Moisten the exposed cake board around the base of the cake and place a few lumps of white fondant on the board at the base of the bag. Knead and roll the remaining white fondant into a long strip about 12 inches (30 cm long). Slice a little off one long edge to neaten and slide your knife underneath the length of the fondant to make sure it's not stuck to your work surface.

18 Starting from the back and with the neat edge against the sack, lay the white fondant around the bag. Gently press it into place and trim and neaten the edge of the board. Roll the leftover bits into snowballs and pile up against the sack (use them also to hide any problems!).

Fig. 1

Fig. 2

CANDY CANE FACTORY CAKE

Ever wondered how a candy cane gets its stripes? Well, now you know!

Ingredients
If using a sponge cake:
8 in (20 cm) round sponge cake
1 quantity of buttercream (see page 24)

If using a fruit cake:
8 in (20 cm) round fruit cake
3-4 tablespoons apricot jam
2 tablespoons of brandy (optional)
1 lb 8 oz (700 g) marzipan (almond paste)

For both types of cake you will also need:
Confectioners' sugar for rolling out fondant on
Water, boiled and cooled for sticking fondant
2 lb 4 oz (1 kg) white fondant
2 oz (60 g) green fondant
1 oz (30 g) black fondant
2 oz (60 g) red fondant
1 oz (30 g) flesh-colored fondant
2/3 oz (20 g) gray fondant
1 strand raw, dried spaghetti
Black food coloring
3 candy canes

Equipment
Carving knife
Palette knife
Rolling pin
Cake smoothers (optional)
Small, sharp, non-serrated knife
Paintbrush
Piping nozzle (tip)—any design
Cheeky straw (see page 11)

CANDY CANE CUPCAKES

To make a mini candy cane, roll about ¹/₈ oz (5 g) of green, red and white fondant into thin strings. Twist them together to form a mulit-colored rope. Cut to length and bend into a cane shape.

How to Make Your Candy Cane Factory Cake

1 If using a sponge cake, level the cake and turn it upside down. Split and fill the middle with buttercream. Reassemble the cake and spread buttercream around the top and sides. Cover it using 1 pound 8 ounces (700 g) white fondant. If using a fruitcake, level the top and place upside down on the board. If you're using brandy, pierce the top with a toothpick a few times and drizzle the brandy over the top. Heat the apricot jam in a microwave in a heatproof bowl for a minute then spread over the top and sides. Cover with the marzipan. Moisten the covered cake with a little water then cover using 1 pound 8 ounces (700 g) of white fondant. Smooth the top and sides and trim around the base.

2 Moisten the exposed board with a little water. Knead and roll about 7 ounces (200 g) of white fondant into a long sausage about 30 inches (76 cm) long. Press and stick it around the base of the cake. It's supposed to look like snow so it can look a little uneven. Cut away any excess icing overhanging the edges of the board.

3 Make a plain candy cane by rolling about 2/3 ounce (20 g) of white fondant into a thick string about 7 inches (18 cm) long. Bend one end round to form a candy cane shape and place to one side to harden. Make two.

4 To make the elf, begin with his legs. (Fig. 1) Roll 1 1/2 ounces (45 g) of green fondant into a sausage about 6 inches (15 cm) long. Slice a little off the two rounded ends and bend it into a "U" shape and stick it onto the top of the cake. Dab a little water onto the end of each leg.

5 Keeping a small piece of the black fondant back to make the paint pot and brush handles later, roll the rest into a sausage about 4 inches (10 cm) long. Cut the sausage in half. Bend each half into an "L" shape using the rounded end to form the foot. Stick the boot onto the end of one of the legs. Repeat with the second. Press three or four lines into the base of each foot with the back of your knife.

6 Roll about 1 1/2 ounces (45 g) of red fondant into an oval for his body and stick onto the legs. Insert a small section of spaghetti if you wish for extra support.

7 Roll about 2/3 ounce (20 g) of flesh-colored fondant into a ball shape for his head and stick on top of the body. Holding the piping nozzle (tip) at an angle, press a smile into the lower part of his face (Fig. 2). Press a smaller curve either side of his mouth with the cheeky straw.

8 Make two tiny slightly flattened white ball shapes for his eyes and stick them onto his face. Add a tiny flesh carrot shape for his nose.

9 Shape about 1/3 ounce (10 g) of green fondant into a carrot shape for his hat. Bend the pointed end over slightly and stick onto the top of his head. Roll about 1/8 ounce (5 g) of white fondant into a thin string and stick around the base of his hat. Make a tiny white fondant ball for the pom pom and stick onto the tip of the hat.

10 Make two tiny flesh-colored carrot shapes for his ears and stick one either side of his head. Press a long indent into each one with the end of your paintbrush. Paint two black food color dots on his eyes.

11 Roll 1/3 ounce (10 g) of red fondant into a sausage about 3 inches (8 cm) long for his arms. Cut it in half and using the rounded end as the shoulder, stick the right arm onto the elf. Bend the arm at the elbow and rest the wrist on the leg.

12 Place a candy cane across his body and over the arm. If the hook section rests on the cake surface it should sit fairly securely. Make a small flesh-colored ball shape for the hand and stick over the candy cane as though he's holding it.

13 Stick the left arm so that the wrist rests on top of the candy cane. Make a second hand to hold it in place

14 To make the paint pots, pull off a tiny bit of gray fondant for the hinges and roll the rest into a thick sausage about 2 inches (5 cm) long. Cut it in half to make the two pots. (Fig. 3) Make a small green fondant ball shape and flatten it. Stick it on top of one of the pots. Make a flat red disc for the second pot. If you want to make a "drip" pinch one edge and pull it into a point so the disc looks a bit like a ping-pong paddle. Stick it on top of the second pot with the drip hanging down the side.

15 Make two tiny black fondant strings for the handles and stick one on either pot. Stick a tiny gray ball on both ends of both handles and poke a hollow into each one with the end of your paintbrush.

16 To make the paintbrushes make two tapering black string shapes and two tiny gray oval shapes for the handles. Make two tiny diamond shapes for the brushes—one red and one green. Press a few lines into each brush head to resemble bristles. Arrange and stick the brushes and pots and a couple of extra candy canes on top of the cake.

Fig. 1

Fig. 2

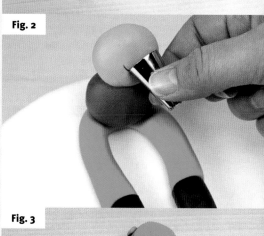

Fig. 3

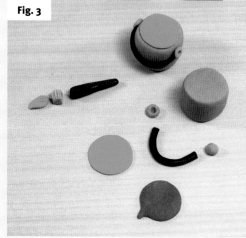

TIPS: *Slightly lessen the amount of work by using one-color candy canes. That way you only need to make one paint pot.*

The elf is supposed to be sitting in the snow so if your cake covering is less than perfect make a few fondant snowballs and use them to hide any problem areas.

SKIING SNOWMAN CAKE

If your cake surface looks less than perfect, hide any problems under small white round fondant "snowballs," extra penguins or fondant fir trees. If you prefer a cake with more action in it, place him on a sloping cake like the one used for Sledding Santa on page 60.

on page 60.

Ingredients
8 in (20 cm) round sponge cake
1 quantity buttercream (see page 24)
or
8 in round fruitcake
3-4 tablespoons apricot jam
1 lb 8 oz (700 g) marzipan (almond paste)

For both types of cake:
2 lb 4 oz (1 kg) white fondant
1 oz (30 g) brown fondant
1/2 oz (15 g) red fondant
1 1/2 oz (45 g) green fondant
1/8 oz (5 g) gray fondant
1/3 oz (10 g) orange-colored fondant
1 oz (30 g) black fondant
Black food coloring
1 strand raw, uncooked spaghetti
Confectioners' sugar for rolling out
 fondant on
Water, boiled and cooled for sticking

Equipment
10 in (25 cm) round cake board
Carving knife
Palette knife
Rolling pin
Cake smoothers (optional)
Small, sharp, non-serrated knife
Plastic wrap
Paintbrushes (medium and fine)
2 toothpicks (cocktail sticks)
Ribbon : 28 in (71 cm) for cake, 33 in (84 cm)
 for the board
Sticky tape
Scissors
Non-toxic glue stick

SKIING SNOWMAN CUPCAKES

Cover the cupcake with either a disc of white fondant or soft white icing (not royal icing). Make a white fondant ball for his body and a smaller one for his head. Make a tiny orange-colored fondant carrot shape for his nose, and paint (or use a toothpick dipped in black food coloring) dots for his eyes, mouth, and buttons. Place a red fondant triangle on his head and stick a thin string of white fondant around the base and finish it off with a white fondant ball on the tip. I then covered him with "snow" by sprinkling a little confectioners' sugar over the top.

How to Make Your Skiing Snowman Cake

Fig. 1

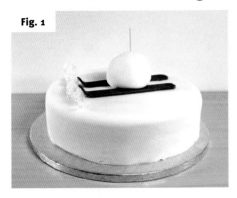

1 If using a sponge cake, level the cake and turn it upside down. Split and fill the middle with buttercream. Reassemble the cake and spread buttercream around the top and sides. Cover using 1 pound 8 ounces (700 g) white fondant. If using a fruitcake, level the top and place upside down on the board. Heat the apricot jam in a microwave in a heatproof bowl for a couple of minutes then spread over the top and sides. Cover with the marzipan. Moisten the covered cake with a little water then cover using 1 pound 8 ounces (700 g) of white fondant.

2 Begin with the skis. Roll the brown fondant into a sausage about 9 inches (23 cm) long and cut in half. Using a rolling pin, flatten both halves to make two thin strips about 5 inches (13 cm) long. Stick both skis on top of the cake with little dabs of water. Gently lift the front of each ski up and support it with scrunched up plastic wrap until it dries (Fig. 1).

3 Make a 5 ounce (150 g) white fondant ball for his body (Fig. 2) and stick on top of the skis. Insert a section of spaghetti for stability if you wish. Make a 1 1/2 ounce (45 g) white fondant

ball for his head and stick onto the body.

4 Shape the red fondant into a triangle for his hat and stick on top of his head. Bend the tip slightly to one side.

5 Roll 1/3 ounce (10 g) white fondant into a sausage about 4 inches (10 cm) long and starting from the back, stick around the base of the hat. Poke a few hollows into the strip with the end of your paintbrush. Make a white ball for the hat's pom pom and stick on the tip of the hat. Poke a few hollows into the pom pom.

6 Make the scarf by thinly rolling out the green fondant and cutting a strip about 7 x 1 inch (18 x 2.5 cm). Press a few lines into the scarf using the back of your knife then stick around the snowman's neck. Keep and cover the left over green fondant.

7 Make the ski pole by threading a small gray fondant ball onto a toothpick. Make two.

8 Roll 1/3 ounce (10 g) of white fondant into a sausage about 2 inches (5 cm) long for his arms. Using a rolling pin, flatten it to produce a flat lozenge shape about 3 inches (8 cm) long. Cut the lozenge in half.

9 Stand one ski pole against the snowman's side with its point in the "snow." Stick one arm against the snowman's body and over the top of the ski pole as though holding it. Repeat on the other side.

10 Re-roll the leftover green fondant and cut out a rectangle about 1 1/2 x 1 inch (4 x 2.5 cm). Press three lines across the rectangle and cut a fringe into one end. Using your paintbrush, carefully pry a section of scarf away from the snowman's neck and tuck the unfringed end of the scarf into this gap. Splay the fringes slightly if you wish.

11 Make two tiny white fondant balls for his

Fig. 3

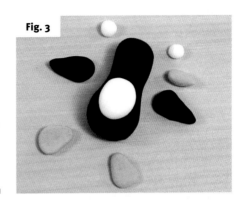

eyes. Squash them and stick them onto his head just below the brim of the hat. Make two black fondant dots and stick one on each eye. Make three larger black dots for his buttons and stick in a line down his tummy.

12 Make a tiny orange fondant carrot shape for his nose. Press a few lines across the carrot and stick onto his face.

13 To make the penguin, make two tiny orange-colored fondant carrot shapes and squash them to form his feet (Fig. 3). Shape 1/3 ounce (10 g) of black fondant into an oval for his body and squeeze the center to form a neck. Stick the feet in position on the cake and stand and stick the body on top.

14 Make two tiny white fondant ball shapes for his eyes and stick onto his head. Make a third white ball, flatten it and stick on to his tummy.

15 Make a tiny orange-colored carrot shape for his beak and stick onto his head. Make two black fondant carrot shapes for his wings. Bend one almost in half and stick on the penguin's shoulder with the pointed tip touching the side of his head. Bend the second wing into an "S" shape and stick on the other side of his body. Paint two black food coloring dots on his eyes to finish

16 Stand ribbon around the base of the cake and secure at the back with a little sticky tape. Glue ribbon around the edge of the board if you wish.

> **TIPS:** If using a sponge cake, don't overfill the center of the cake with buttercream. The snowman is fairly heavy and his weight could cause the cake to sink slightly.
>
> As Christmas is a busy time, you could make the snowman in advance and place on a thin cake card like the pram on Baby's First Birthday Cake. Hide the cardboard edges with snowballs..

Fig. 2

SNOWFLAKE CUPCAKES

These edible wafer paper snowflakes are an easy way to make seasonal cupcakes. If you're making them for a birthday then why stop at snowflakes? Cut letters out of colored wafer paper and spell the birthday person's name in cupcakes too!

Ingredients
12 cupcakes (recipe page 22)
2 quantities of soft white frosting (see page 25)
1 pack of white edible wafer paper
Blue food color

Equipment
Pencil
Ruler
Scissors
Bowl
Spoon or palette knife for stirring
Piping bag
Large star nozzle (tip)

> **TIPS:** *You can frost your snowflakes by painting a light line of water around the edges of the snowflake and dipping them into confectioners' sugar. Lay them flat until they have dried out and you can lift them safely.*
>
> *You could sift some confectioners' sugar "snow" over the finished cupcakes. Place a little sugar in a sieve and gently tap over the top.*

How to Make Your Snowflake Cupcakes

1 Begin with the snowflakes. Cut a sheet of edible wafer paper into squares – the size you want your snowflakes to be. Mine were quite large about 3 inches (8 cm) or so.
2 Fold the sheet in half to make a rectangle (Fig. 1).

3 Fold the paper in half again to make a square. Now you need to cut two triangles out of the square. It may be useful to draw guidelines in pencil for the first few (Fig. 2).
4 Snip little shapes out of the edges (Fig. 3).

5 Carefully unfold the paper to reveal your snowflake.
6 Color your white frosting a light blue by stirring in a dash of blue food coloring.
7 Place into the piping bag. Pipe a swirl onto a cupcake and place a snowflake on top.

Fig. 1

Fig. 2

Fig. 3

A WINTER CASTLE CAKE

Ideal for Christmas (and birthdays), a wonderful winter castle that is incredibly easy to make. As the paper is fairly thin the cake would look good back lit by fairy lights. Avoid candles though....

Ingredients

If using a sponge cake :
8 in (20 cm) round sponge cake
2 quantities soft white frosting (see page 25)

If using a fruitcake:

8 in round fruitcake
3-4 tablespoons apricot jam
1 lb 8 oz (700 g) marzipan (almond paste)
2 quantities white royal icing (see page 24)

For both cakes you will also need:

5-6 sheets of white edible paper
2 sheets of blue-colored edible paper (see TIPS)
4 oz (120 g) dark green fondant
Confectioners' sugar for rolling out fondant on and for making "snow"

Equipment

10 in (25 cm) round cake board
Castle Templates (pages 74, 76, and 77)
Black food color pen
Scissors
Ruler
Toothpick (cocktail stick)
Carving knife
Palette knife
Small sharp nail scissors
Piping bag and no. 2 piping nozzle (tip) (optional—it make things a bit easier using a piping bag but you can just smear a little on the top of the turret with a knife)
Teaspoon
Tea strainer or small sieve

TIPS: *You can make your own colored wafer paper by rubbing a little cocoa or colored cake dusting powder onto the paper or you can buy different colors of edible paper*
Keep the castle away from candles. If you have time you could add some penguins frolicking in the snow outside the castle walls.

Fig. 1

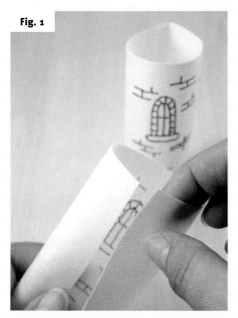

1 Begin by making the castle sections so that they can have a little time to set before positioning them on the cake. Place a sheet of edible paper over one of the wall templates and trace over it using the food color pen. Cut it out and place to one side. Trace and cut out four short turrets and one taller one. Also, cut out one center section, five blue roofs and five white flags.

2 Take a turret, and paint a light line of water down one edge. Bend the other edge round to meet the first and press the two edges together (Fig. 1). The paper should now form a tube. Repeat with the other four turrets and the center section.

3 Bend a roof round to form a cone shape (Fig. 2). Again glue the seam with a light dab of water. Repeat on the other four roofs.

4 Make the fir trees so they're ready to pop

on the cake. Take about ½ ounce (15 g) of the dark green fondant and roll it into a carrot shape. Poke a toothpick into the base to make it easy to hold then make little partial snips around the tree with the nail scissors (see page 63). Make about 10 trees and place to one side.

5 Level the cake and turn it upside down. You could cut a few irregular chunks out of the cake to make it look mountainous.

6 If you are using a fruitcake, spread the apricot jam around the sides and cover with the marzipan. Then spread royal icing thickly over the cake and exposed cake board. If you are using a sponge cake, split and fill with white frosting then reassemble the cake and spread a liberal coating of white frosting over the outside of the cake and the exposed board.

7 Stand the short round center section in the middle of the cake. Take the longest turret and pipe or smear a little icing around the top edge. Place a roof on top and stand in the middle of the center section. Repeat using the

Fig. 2

Fig. 3

other four turrets and stand these around the outside of the center section.

8 Check everything is standing securely. You can always pile extra frosting up against the turrets to hold them in place. It'll just look like a snowdrift!

9 Carefully press the fir trees into the snow around the castle.

10 Pipe or apply a dab of frosting to the top of a roof and stand a flag in it. The paper flag should be small and light enough to stand upright.

11 To finish, place a little confectioners' sugar into a tea strainer or small sieve and gently tap over the roofs and trees.

WINTER CASTLE CUPCAKES

Place a piece of edible wafer paper over the small castle template on page 76. Trace over it with an edible food pen and cut it out. Bend round and stick the join together with a light dab of water. Cut out three tiny food wafer triangles for flags and stick one on the top of each roof with a tiny dab of water. Pipe a swirl of buttercream on the top of the cupcake and gently press the castle into position. Finish with candies, sprinkles, or edible silver balls.

Templates (all templates actual size)

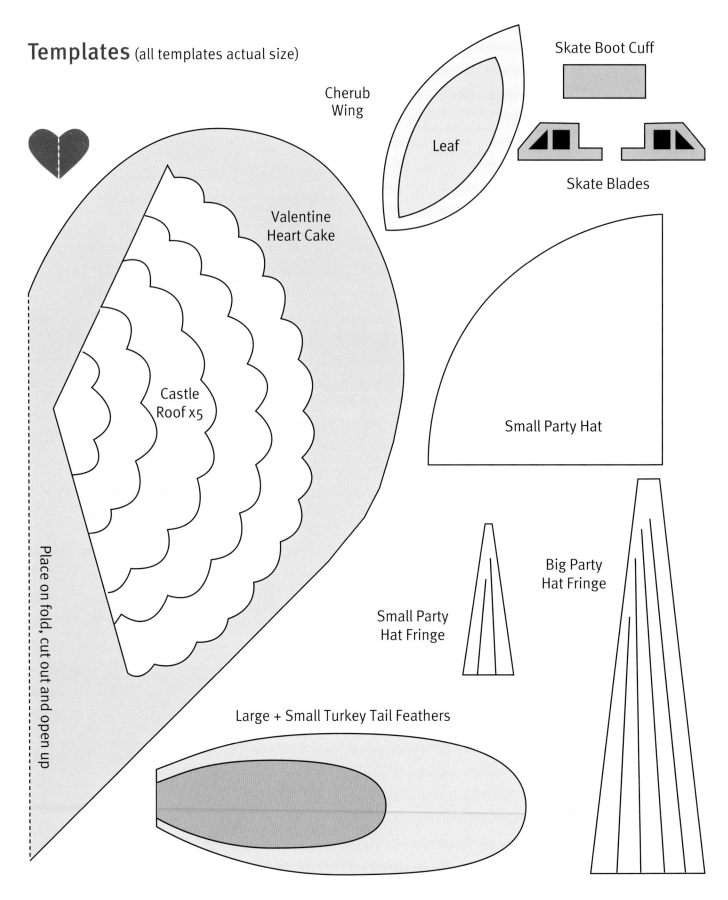

Cherub Wing

Skate Boot Cuff

Leaf

Skate Blades

Valentine Heart Cake

Small Party Hat

Castle Roof x5

Place on fold, cut out and open up

Small Party Hat Fringe

Big Party Hat Fringe

Large + Small Turkey Tail Feathers

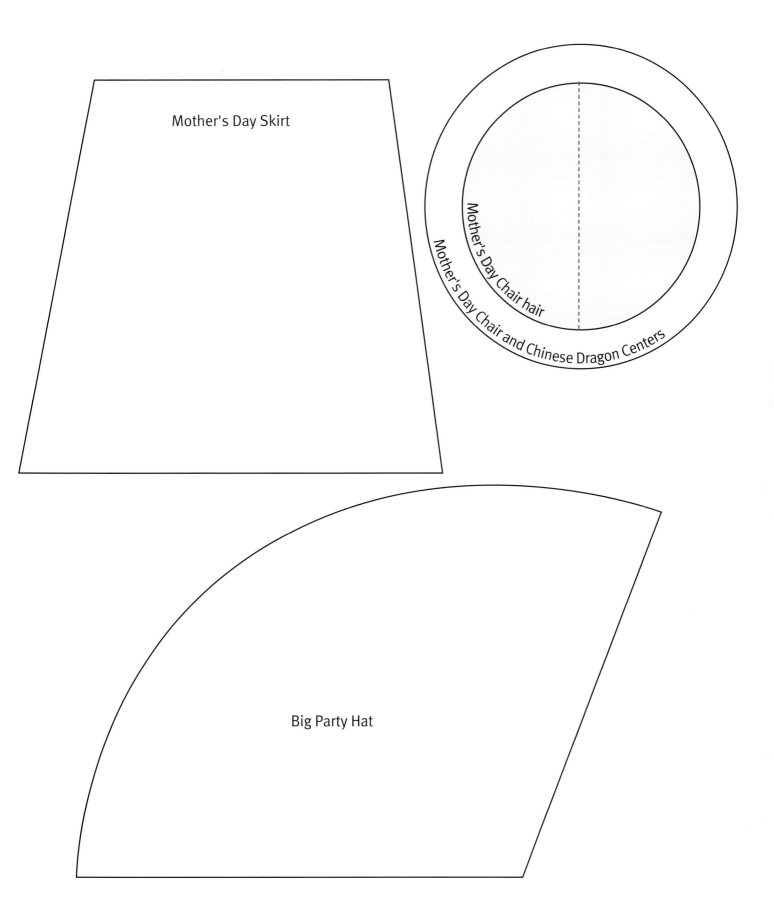

Mother's Day Skirt

Mother's Day Chair hair

Mother's Day Chair and Chinese Dragon Centers

Big Party Hat

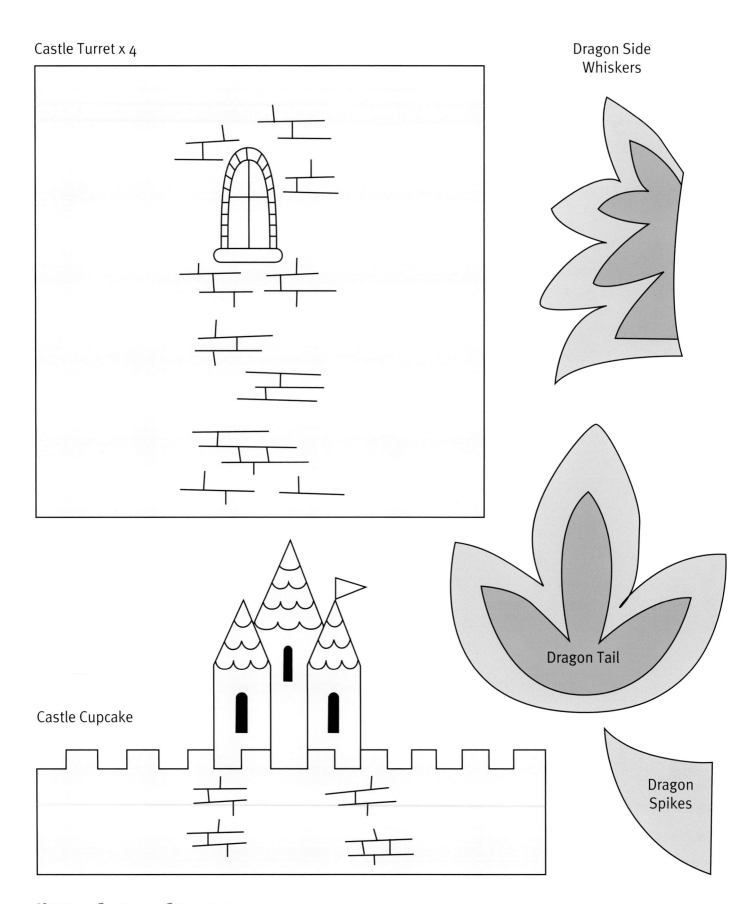

Castle Turret x 4

Dragon Side
Whiskers

Dragon Tail

Dragon
Spikes

Castle Cupcake

Central Castle Turret x 1

Central Castle Section

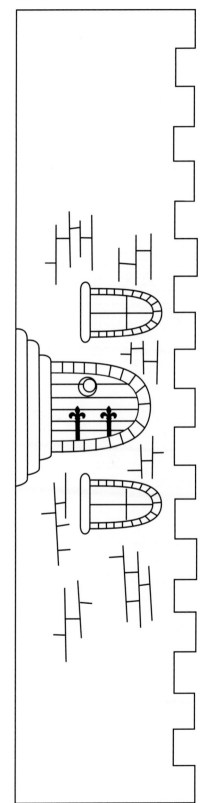

Dragon Eyebrows + Whiskers

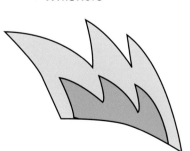

Castle Flags x5

Dragon Teeth

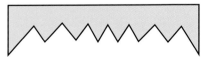

Fondant Sizing Guide

These guides will give you a rough idea of the size of balls of fondant you will need if you don't possess a set of scales.

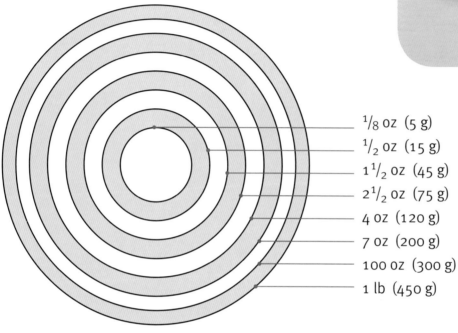

$\frac{1}{8}$ oz (5 g)

$\frac{1}{2}$ oz (15 g)

$1\frac{1}{2}$ oz (45 g)

$2\frac{1}{2}$ oz (75 g)

4 oz (120 g)

7 oz (200 g)

100 oz (300 g)

1 lb (450 g)

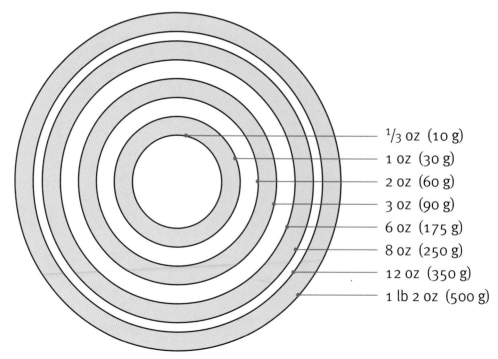

$\frac{1}{3}$ oz (10 g)

1 oz (30 g)

2 oz (60 g)

3 oz (90 g)

6 oz (175 g)

8 oz (250 g)

12 oz (350 g)

1 lb 2 oz (500 g)

Making a Piping Bag

1 Make a greaseproof paper triangle and lay it flat with the point towards you. Fold "C" over to form a cone shape.

2 Wrap "A" around the cone. Points "A" and "C" should meet together at the back and the tip of the cone should be pointed.

3 Fold "A" and "C" over a couple of times to hold the bag together. If using a piping nozzle (tip) cut a little off the point and place the nozzle (tip) inside followed by some buttercream. If you are not using a nozzle just place buttercream inside the bag. Fold the top over to close the bag and cut a tiny triangle off the point ready for piping.

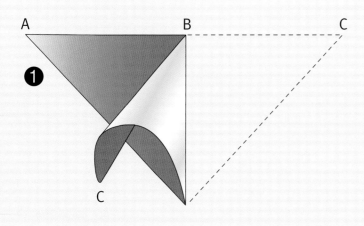

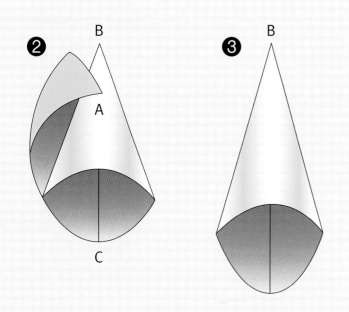

Suppliers

If you have trouble obtaining cake equipment or materials including fondant (sugarpaste) one of the following companies may be able to help.

UK

Culpitt Ltd
Jubilee Industrial Estate
Ashington
Northumberland
NE63 8UQ
UK
Tel: +44 (0) 1670 814545
www.culpitt.com

Design a Cake
30 / 31 Phoenix Road,
Crowther Industrial Estate,
Washington,
Tyne & Wear,
NE38 0AD
UK
Sales: +44(0)191 417 1572
Enquiries +44(0) 1914179697
www.design-a-cake.co.uk

Renshawnapier Limited
Crown street
Liverpool
L8 7RF
Tel 0151 706 8200
www.renshawnapier.co.uk

Squires Kitchen
3 Waverley Lane
Farnham
Surrey
GU9 8BB
UK
Tel: +44 (0)1252 260 260
www.squires-shop.com

USA

Beryl's Cake Decorating & Pastry Supplies
PO Box 1584
North Springfield, VA 22151
Tel: 1-800-488-2749
Fax: (703) 750-3779
www.beryls.com

Wilton
Wilton Industries
2240 W 75th St
Woodridge
IL 60517
Tel: 630-963-1818 or
     800-794-5866
www.wilton.com

If you have any problems or get stuck contact me:
http://caroldeaconcakes.com

Index

The Tuttle Story: "Books to Span the East and West"

Most people are surprised to learn that the world's largest publisher of books on Asia had its humble beginnings in the tiny American state of Vermont. The company's founder, Charles E. Tuttle, belonged to a New England family steeped in publishing. And his first love was naturally books—especially old and rare editions.

Immediately after WW II, serving in Tokyo under General Douglas MacArthur, Tuttle was tasked with reviving the Japanese publishing industry. He later founded the Charles E. Tuttle Publishing Company, which thrives today as one of the world's leading independent publishers.

Though a westerner, Tuttle was hugely instrumental in bringing a knowledge of Japan and Asia to a world hungry for information about the East. By the time of his death in 1993, Tuttle had published over 6,000 books on Asian culture, history and art—a legacy honored by the Japanese emperor with the "Order of the Sacred Treasure," the highest tribute Japan can bestow upon a non-Japanese.

With a backlist of 1,500 titles, Tuttle Publishing is more active today than at any time in its past—inspired by Charles Tuttle's core mission to publish fine books to span the East and West and provide a greater understanding of each.